D0759956

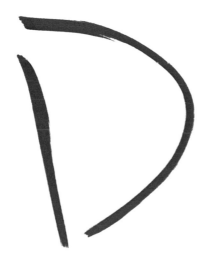

TEEN LIFE 411™

DRINKING AND DRIVING.

NOW WHAT?

VALERIE MENDRALLA

AND

JANET GROSSHANDLER

ROSEN
PUBLISHING®

New York

This book is dedicated to the young people who seek out and use knowledge to become empowered to resist peer pressure, serve as role models, and educate their fellow peers.

Published in 2012 by The Rosen Publishing Group, Inc.
29 East 21st Street, New York, NY 10010

First Edition

Library of Congress Cataloging-in-Publication Data

Mendralla, Valerie.
Drinking and driving, now what? / Valerie Mendralla, Janet Grosshandler.—1st ed.
    p. cm.—(Teen life 411)
Includes bibliographical references and index.
ISBN 978-1-4488-4654-2 (library binding)
1. Drinking and traffic accidents—United States—Juvenile litera-
ture. 2. Drunk driving—United States—Juvenile literature. 3.
Teenagers—Alcohol use—United States—Juvenile literature. I.
Grosshandler, Janet. II. Title. III. Title: Drinking and driving.
HE5620.D72M46 2012
363.12'51708350973—dc22
                                                              2010042037

Manufactured in the United States of America

CPSIA Compliance Information: Batch #S11YA: For further information, contact Rosen Publishing, New York, New York, at 1-800-237-9932.

CONTENTS

Learning how to drive has long been considered a milestone of the adolescent years. Also, teenagers experimenting with and abusing alcohol is nothing new. However, combining the two makes for a tragic mix of poor decision making, car crashes, injuries, legal problems, and potentially life-changing situations.

As a way to prevent such tragedies, the legal drinking age has been raised, and the limit for blood alcohol concentration has been lowered. New driver restrictions are abundant, and fines have never been heavier. Research suggests that changing policies can be an effective prevention strategy. In the last decade, there has been a significant decline in crash rates and impaired driving among teens.

Terminology has also changed. You may still hear people talk about "car accidents" on the road, and this

Most crashes are preventable and predictable. This book serves as a tool to gain knowledge about preventing such tragedies.

might be how you would speak of them as well. The government pushed to make the transition from "accident" to "crash." The reason for this change is that a crash is predictable and preventable. An accident is not. Most of the crashes that occur are, in fact, preventable and predictable: The driver was speeding, texting, eating, or drinking; the driver was distracted by passengers in the car, etc. Be observant—listen to how news anchors, radio personalities, and others talk about traffic safety. You may begin to notice that you hear the phrase "car accident" less often. Spread the word by educating your family and friends.

Adolescence is a time of acceptance, belonging, and, sometimes, rebellion. Teens usually make their decisions based on their perception of what others their age are doing. For example, choices such as what you watch on television, the music you listen to, how you dress, and how you manage your time are usually influenced by friends rather than your parents. The establishment of peer-led groups has worked to take advantage of this phenomenon. Teens talking to other teens about safe driving and having fun without alcohol can be very effective in changing attitudes and perceptions and, in turn, behaviors.

This book serves as a tool for teens. By seeing the whole picture—statistics, laws, real-life stories, and ways to help—teens will be empowered to make responsible decisions about drinking and driving.

THE HIGH COST of DRINKING AND DRIVING

According to the National Highway Traffic Safety Administration (NHTSA), three out of ten people in the United States will be involved in an alcohol-related car crash at some time in their lives. Think about this at your next family gathering. Imagine three of your family members on one side of a room and seven family members on the other side. Look at the side that has the three family members. Those are the people who, according to the NHTSA statistic, will be in an alcohol-related car crash. For some of them, it will mean injuries and a stay in the hospital. For others, it could mean death. A drunk driver whom you do not know may hit your loved ones. Or, it may be a family member who gets drunk and becomes responsible for injuring or killing someone else.

Drinking and driving can destroy lives and families. In addition to these human costs, there are also steep monetary costs associated with drinking and driving. These include medical bills, property damage, the expenses that accumulate when someone is disabled and can no longer work, and other direct expenditures. According to the Underage Drinking Enforcement Training Center (UDETC), the

NHTSA estimates that three out of ten Americans will be involved in an alcohol-related crash at some point in their lives.

estimated cost of youth alcohol-related crashes in the United States in 2007 was $10 billion.

Drinking and driving has devastating effects on the entire nation. At the very least, people who drink and drive can lose their privileges to drive. At worst, they can lose their loved ones or even their lives. Billions of dollars are spent each year in an effort to prevent alcohol-related crashes and educate young men and women about making good decisions.

DEATH BY NUMBERS

Tragically, thousands of Americans learn the same terrible lesson every year: alcohol and driving do not mix. Here are some startling statistics from NHTSA:

- Some 5,864 drivers between the ages of fifteen and twenty were involved in fatal motor vehicle crashes in 2008.
- Of the fifteen to twenty year olds involved in fatal crashes in 2008, 31 percent of the drivers had been drinking.
- The number of teens involved in fatal car crashes has decreased 27 percent from 1998 to 2008. Although the rate is declining, motor vehicle crashes continue to be the leading cause of death for teens.

The decrease in motor vehicle crashes among teens does not mean that drinking and driving is not a serious problem. Thousands of teens are killed or seriously injured in alcohol-related crashes each year. Teens who get behind the wheel after drinking may also hurt innocent bystanders or other drivers.

No matter how old you are or how much driving experience you have, drinking and driving is always dangerous. However, your chances of being in a motor vehicle crash increase when you get into a car with a teen driver, rather than an adult driver. Teens have less driving experience than adults. As a result, they have a greater risk of being in a collision, even without the

Driver Fatalities and Drivers Involved in Fatal Crashes Among 15- to 20-Year-Old Drivers, 1998-2008

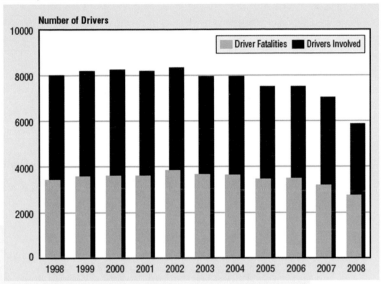

The number of teen drivers involved in fatal crashes decreased from 1998 to 2008, according to NHTSA. Still, 2,739 teen drivers were killed and 5,864 were involved in deadly crashes in 2008.

influence of alcohol. If the teenager has been drinking, the risk of a crash is even higher.

Although drinking and driving occurs among teens of both sexes, statistics indicate that boys are more likely to be involved in fatal crashes in which alcohol is a factor. NHTSA reports that in 2008, crashes among drivers between fifteen and twenty years of age were more likely to have involved alcohol if the driver was male. Twenty-six percent of male drivers ages sixteen to twenty involved in fatal crashes were drinking at the time, as compared to 13 percent of female drivers in the same age group.

The use of seat belts is also a factor in the outcome of alcohol-related car crashes. Wearing a seat belt can increase your chances of surviving a crash. When drinking, teens are less likely to wear seat belts. According to NHTSA, 73 percent of young drivers who were involved in fatal alcohol-related crashes in 2008 were not wearing seat belts. The drunk driver is often not the victim in the crash that he or she has caused. Many times, it is the passenger who is killed because he or she did not wear a seat belt.

THE EFFECTS OF ALCOHOL

Many teens do not consider alcohol to be a harmful drug. In many families, adults drink wine with meals or have a beer after work. Perhaps you are allowed a sip of champagne on family holidays. Alcohol is socially acceptable and often plays a part in celebrating happy times and religious events. However, when alcohol is not used responsibly, it can have devastating effects.

Alcohol affects the central nervous system and brain, which in turn affects the entire body. In small doses, alcohol can give one a feeling of being happy, silly, and energetic. When taken in larger doses, it is a depressant, and it slows down all bodily functions.

Alcohol enters the bloodstream directly without being digested. Researchers say that small amounts are absorbed directly through the lining of the mouth and throat. Most of the alcohol goes through the walls of the stomach and small intestine and is absorbed into the blood. From there, it travels to the brain and other organs of the body. How drunk a person gets depends on his or her age, weight, and gender, how fast he or she drinks, and how much food is in the stomach.

Most of the alcohol that a person drinks is processed in the liver. Enzymes in the liver break down the alcohol, and it eventually leaves the body as carbon dioxide and water. The rest is eliminated through breath, sweat, and urine. The body breaks down alcohol slowly. If a person drinks more than he or she can eliminate, the drug accumulates in the body. The person becomes intoxicated, which means that the poisonous or toxic effects of alcohol go into action in the brain and the body. As a result, the person feels drunk.

THE ROLE OF PEER PRESSURE

Peer pressure can play an important role in teen drinking. Often, it is because of peer pressure that a teenager will drink at a party, even though he or she did not plan to drink. It is usually because of peer pressure that teens drink a lot more than their bodies can handle. When it's time to leave a party, finding a sober driver can be tough. It is hard for someone to admit that he or she has had too much and shouldn't drive. Drinking impairs a person's judgment: a teen may not even realize that he or she is too drunk to drive. An intoxicated person might become angry if others suggest that he or she should not drive. More often than not, teens will get behind the wheel—or into someone else's car—when they shouldn't.

ASK DR. JAN, PSYCHOLOGIST

First name: Amy

Question:
I'm a sophomore, and I like attending the football games at my high school. For the past few games, I've noticed a group of senior guys from my school sneak in alcohol and drink it in the bleachers. Other students have noticed, too, but they think it's funny. I assume the guys are drinking and driving, since they drive themselves to the game. Do I have an obligation to tell someone? Whom should I tell? I don't want to be called a snitch.

Answer:
We know from research that as high school students get older, their experimentation with alcohol increases. It would not be surprising, therefore, that seniors at your school drink more than younger students. We also know that some high school students—and even middle school students—sneak alcohol into sporting events or bring alcohol to school, often in water or soda bottles. Too often, these students drink so much that they end up passing out, and they need to be rushed to the emergency room. Often, students underestimate how dangerous alcohol can be because it is legal. Most people don't know that, because of their higher rate of metabolism, teenagers actually need to drink more alcohol than adults in order to feel the intoxicating effects. Thus, alcohol poisoning is a very serious problem among high school students nationwide.

While you do not have an obligation to tell someone, you would be doing your fellow students a great favor by doing so. Chances are the seniors that are sneaking in alcohol do not realize they are exposing themselves to a life-threatening risk. You would be doing your school a great service by letting your principal know. I would also suggest that you let administrators know in writing and keep a copy because that will increase the odds that they will address the issue. Better yet, consider having one of your parents do so, as this may also increase the odds that they will follow through on this potentially deadly problem. In terms of being a snitch, you don't have to tell them specifically who is drinking. However, if you have specific concerns about certain students, letting the principal know will increase the odds that these students will get the help that they may need, including support in making healthier choices in the future.

Ask a Question

Do you have a question that you would like answered? E-mail your question to Dr. Jan at drjan@rosenpub.com. If your question is selected, it will appear on the Teen Health & Wellness Web site in "Dr. Jan's Corner."

If you have an urgent question on a health or wellness issue, we strongly encourage you to call a hotline to speak to a qualified professional or speak to a trusted adult, such as a parent, teacher, or guidance counselor. You can find hotlines listed in the For More Information section of this book, or at www. teenhealthandwellness.com/static/hotlines.

Getting behind the wheel of a car after a few drinks may not seem like a big deal. "It's only a few blocks," you might reason. "I'll drive slowly and be extra careful." However, the drive doesn't have to be long for a tragedy to occur. If there is a crash, many people besides you will be affected. The passengers in other cars may be hurt or killed. Their families and friends will feel anger and pain over their loss. Losing a child,

Peer pressure often plays an important role when it comes to drinking alcohol and getting behind the wheel of a car after drinking.

parent, or friend is something that scars a person for life. Giving in to peer pressure to drink, driving after you've been drinking, and riding with a drunk driver are dangerous choices.

What can you do about the problem of drinking and driving? You can designate a driver when you go to parties. You can stop a friend who has been drinking from getting behind the wheel. Alternatively, you can call an adult, sibling, or friend to pick you up when you've had too much to drink. Never get into a car with a driver who has been drinking. These are just a few ways to protect yourself and others from the tragedies caused by drinking and driving. This book will discuss other ways to fight the problem of drinking and driving. Too many lives have already been lost.

CHAPTER 2

HOW ALCOHOL AFFECTS THE BODY AND BRAIN

Some people claim they can drive perfectly well after a few drinks. However, studies of the effects of alcohol on driving skills show that this is not the case. You may not feel as if your driving is impaired after you have been drinking, but that doesn't mean you are capable of operating a car, motorcycle, or other vehicle safely. After all, the drunken drivers involved in serious crashes probably didn't expect to crash when they first got on the road. They thought they were doing fine. Then they spun out of control, smashed into an oncoming vehicle, or ran into a telephone pole. To understand why drinking and driving is so dangerous, one must learn how alcohol affects a person's body, brain, and driving ability.

FROM THE BLOOD TO THE BRAIN

Once alcohol is absorbed into the bloodstream, it works to slow the functioning of the central nervous system. The central nervous system includes the brain and spinal cord, and it controls almost all of the body's functions.

"Blood alcohol content" (BAC) is an important term that is used frequently in this book.

BAC refers to the amount of alcohol in a person's blood. As more alcohol is taken in, the percentage of alcohol in the blood rises. Drivers with high blood alcohol content are at a greatly increased risk for crashes, injuries, and deaths on the road.

BAC is always written as a decimal part of 1 percent. For example, if a person has a BAC of 0.1 percent, it means the person has one part alcohol to one thousand parts of blood in his or her body. BAC can be measured using a breath, blood, or urine test.

As a person's BAC rises, the effects of alcohol become more pronounced. To show what happens to people when blood alcohol content rises, researchers have described five levels of intoxication:

- **Level 1:** A person has a moderate amount to drink (about one drink for women or two drinks for men) in a period of one to two hours. The person's blood alcohol content is in the range of .01 to .05 percent. At this stage, the alcohol may make a person feel happy, relaxed, talkative, flirty, and confident. However, if the person has a BAC of more than .03 percent, his or her driving skills are already affected.

- **Level 2:** Continuing to drink will boost the blood alcohol content to between .05 and .08 percent. Alcohol reaches farther into the higher learning center of the brain. While the person may feel and act self-confident, his or her reaction time, judgment, senses, and movement are impaired.

- **Level 3:** When the blood alcohol content reaches .08 to .15 percent, the person is in a risky state. Thoughts can become muddled, and speech can become slurred. Vision and hearing are affected as well. Balance, coordination, and muscle control are impaired, sometimes resulting in a staggered walk. The individual may have nausea or vomiting. At or above .08 BAC, a person is considered legally intoxicated. Driving with a BAC of .08 or greater is illegal for adults older than twenty-one in the United States. It is unlawful for drivers under twenty-one to have any amount of alcohol in their blood.

- **Level 4:** From .15 to .30 BAC, the person is in a high-risk state. All physical and mental functions are impaired considerably. The person is unable to walk without help. Breathing is labored, body temperature may go down, and reflexes are depressed. There may be a loss of bladder control. The person does not know what he or she is doing or saying and is unable to remember events. Loss of consciousness may occur.

- **Level 5:** Above a .30 BAC, a person is unconscious or in a coma. The part of the brain that controls breathing and heartbeat is dangerously affected. The person is close to death and could die without medical attention.

Using charts developed by researchers, one can estimate a person's BAC without taking a test. The following examples show you how to calculate BAC. Keep in mind that the phrase "one drink" refers to these standard servings: 12 ounces (355 ml) of beer, 5 ounces (148 ml) of wine, and 1.5 ounces (30 ml) of hard liquor. All of these contain about the same amount of alcohol. Be aware that one glass or container, depending on its size, can contain more than one serving of alcohol. How to use the BAC charts:

1. Locate the chart for either men or women on page 22. Given a person's weight and the number of drinks consumed, the chart provides a number.

Example: A 180-pound (81.6-kilogram) man had four drinks. The men's chart says his number is .08.

2. Next, figure out the amount of alcohol already eliminated using the average of .015 per hour for men, or .018 per hour for women.

Example: The man consumed all four drinks within one hour. So .015 x 1 hour = 0.015.

3. Take the first number and subtract the second number.

Example: .08 − .015

The answer is the person's current BAC.

Example: .08 − .015 = .07 BAC.

ESTIMATING BAC

ESTIMATING BAC (CONTINUED)

4. Since we know the approximate rate of elimination, we can figure out how many hours it will take to return to a 0.0 BAC. Take the final BAC calculation and subtract .015 for men and .018 for women; multiply by 60. The answer is in number of hours.

Example: .07 BAC − .015 = .055 x 60 = 3.3 hours

It will take the man 3.3 hours to become sober if no more drinks are consumed.

The BAC charts show rough averages only. Many factors affect the rate of alcohol absorption into the bloodstream. For example, the kind and amount of food and drink consumed, the percentage of fatty tissue in the body, and even the person's ethnicity are all factors that can cause BAC values to vary.

According to the National Institute on Alcohol Abuse and Alcoholism (NIAAA), a standard drink is any drink that contains about 1.2 tablespoons (17.7 ml) of pure alcohol, or ethanol. The chart below illustrates the serving size that counts as "one drink" for four different beverages.

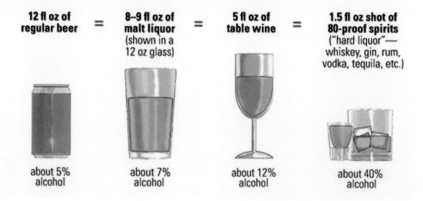

| 12 fl oz of regular beer | = | 8–9 fl oz of malt liquor (shown in a 12 oz glass) | = | 5 fl oz of table wine | = | 1.5 fl oz shot of 80-proof spirits ("hard liquor"— whiskey, gin, rum, vodka, tequila, etc.) |

about 5% alcohol — about 7% alcohol — about 12% alcohol — about 40% alcohol

When looking at the different levels of intoxication and the BAC charts, it is clear that there is no safe way to drive after drinking. This information shows that just a few drinks can create an unsafe driver. It also shows that some people can reach unsafe BAC numbers very quickly. For example, a female of 110 pounds (49.8 kg) needs much less alcohol than her boyfriend of 170 pounds (77.1 kg) to reach the higher levels of intoxication.

In addition, the only thing that can sober a person up is time. The body needs hours to eliminate the alcohol consumed. Nothing can speed up that process. Drinking tons of coffee will only make you wide-awake and drunk, not sober. Cold showers will make you shivering, wet, and drunk. The only way to sober up is to give the liver time to metabolize and get rid of the alcohol.

How Alcohol Affects Driving Ability

Driving requires many skills, sharp senses, lots of concentration, and quick reaction time. Drivers who have been drinking are not effective at putting it all together. Those between the ages of sixteen and nineteen are four times more likely to crash than older drivers, according to the Insurance Institute for Highway Safety. In single-vehicle crashes, NHTSA estimates the relative risk of a driver with a BAC between .08 and .10 is at least eleven times greater than a person's risk with a BAC of 0.0. The risk is fifty-two times greater for young males with that

BAC Table for Men

Drinks	Body Weight in Pounds								Condition
	100	120	140	160	180	200	220	240	
0	.00	.00	.00	.00	.00	.00	.00	.00	Only Safe Driving Limit
1	.04	.03	.03	.02	.02	.02	.02	.02	Driving Skills Significantly Affected
2	.08	.06	.05	.05	.04	.04	.03	.03	
3	.11	.09	.08	.07	.06	.06	.05	.05	
4	.15	.12	.11	.09	.08	.08	.07	.06	Possible Criminal Penalties
5	.19	.16	.13	.12	.11	.09	.09	.08	
6	.23	.19	.16	.14	.13	.11	.10	.09	Legally Intoxicated
7	.26	.22	.19	.16	.15	.13	.12	.11	
8	.30	.25	.21	.19	.17	.15	.14	.13	Criminal Penalties
9	.34	.28	.24	.21	.19	.17	.15	.14	
10	.38	.31	.27	.23	.21	.19	.17	.16	Death Possible

Subtract .01% for each 40 minutes of drinking.
1 drink = 1.25 oz. 80 proof liquor, 12 oz. beer, or 5 oz. wine.

BAC Table for Women

Drinks	Body Weight in Pounds									Condition
	90	100	120	140	160	180	200	220	240	
0	.00	.00	.00	.00	.00	.00	.00	.00	.00	Only Safe Driving Limit
1	.05	.05	.04	.03	.03	.03	.02	.02	.02	Driving Skills Significantly Affected
2	.10	.09	.08	.07	.06	.05	.05	.04	.04	
3	.15	.14	.11	.10	.09	.08	.07	.06	.06	
4	.20	.18	.15	.13	.11	.10	.09	.08	.08	
5	.25	.23	.19	.16	.14	.13	.11	.10	.09	Possible Criminal Penalties
6	.30	.27	.23	.19	.17	.15	.14	.12	.11	Legally Intoxicated
7	.35	.32	.27	.23	.20	.18	.16	.14	.13	
8	.40	.36	.30	.26	.23	.20	.18	.17	.15	Criminal Penalties
9	.45	.41	.34	.29	.26	.23	.20	.19	.17	
10	.51	.45	.38	.32	.28	.25	.23	.21	.19	Death Possible

Subtract .01% for each 40 minutes of drinking.
1 drink = 1.25 oz. 80 proof liquor, 12 oz. beer, or 5 oz. wine.

blood alcohol level. The following paragraphs explain how alcohol impairs every skill you need to drive safely.

Vision

Drinking alcohol affects a driver's vision. Since alcohol is a depressant, it relaxes all the muscles in the body. A person under the influence of alcohol has less control over his or her muscles, including those that move and focus the eyes.

When the eye is working properly, light enters through the pupil and goes through the lens. The lens focuses light rays on the retina. If something interferes with this process, the impulses, or messages, that are sent to the brain are distorted. If a fuzzy picture is sent to the brain, the mind cannot correctly interpret the traffic scene in view.

Alcohol also affects eye focus. A muscle in the eye automatically brings into focus objects both near and far. With the relaxing effect of alcohol, that muscle cannot function properly. Therefore, the person does not see clearly; what he or she sees is blurry.

In addition, alcohol affects how the eyes react to light. The pupil of the eye acts like the shutter of a camera to let in just the right amount of light. The pupil

BAC is affected by a number of factors, including gender, weight, and number of alcoholic drinks consumed. Remember, just a few drinks can create an unsafe driver.

Inability to focus and react to light, double vision, impaired depth perception, and impaired peripheral vision are all examples of how alcohol affects sight.

narrows when bright light enters the eye in order to prevent damage to the retina. In the dark, the pupil opens to admit more light, making it easier for a person to see. When a person is driving at night and the headlights of oncoming cars shine into his or her eyes, it takes one second for the pupils to contract and seven seconds for them to adapt again to the dark. When a person is drinking, the process doesn't happen as quickly. The pupils contract, but it takes them longer to recover. As a result, one can be driving semiblind for several seconds.

Drinking alcohol can lead to double vision. Six muscles act to make the eyes work together. When these muscles are impaired by alcohol, it is difficult for the eyes to focus on the same point. Double vision can result. It may look like two cars are approaching instead of one. Which of the two cars do you avoid?

In addition, the eyes need to work together to judge distances. Changing lanes, passing other cars, and many other driving skills depend on how well a person can judge distances. When a person is drunk, no clearly coordinated picture is sent to the brain. Depth perception is altered. One has difficulty deciding exactly how far away that other car is.

Finally, alcohol affects one's peripheral vision, or the ability to see things outside the central area of focus. Being able to see cars coming out of intersections or driveways and reacting when people walk into the road are crucial abilities when driving. If you notice fewer dangers on either side of you as you drive, you increase your chances of having a motor vehicle crash. Speed also affects peripheral vision. The faster you drive, the less peripheral vision you have. Add the effects of alcohol and you get a driver who sees almost nothing besides the blurry, distorted scene right in front of him or her.

Concentration and Observation

Driving requires a person to monitor many things at once. His or her attention is divided among the many tasks and skills needed to drive safely. A new driver is inexperienced at mentally processing all the information gathered as he or she drives. In addition to all the things a driver needs to accomplish, add the effects of a loud radio, talking on a cell phone, or distractions from passengers. The brain must analyze all of this incoming data. The driver makes and executes decisions based on the brain's conclusions. Alcohol makes it much harder for the driver to manage multiple streams of information effectively and react appropriately. The driver who has been drinking will find it difficult to sort out distractions and focus on the most important thing: driving.

Continual observation of everything in the field of vision—other cars moving in one's direction, stoplights, traffic signs, parked cars, pedestrians, motorcycles, bicycles, and road conditions—is vital to safety. A driver must always be alert: careful observation can be the difference between a safe ride home and a crash. A person uses visual search and recognition skills to sort out all that he or she encounters while driving.

Just looking through the windshield isn't enough to take in all that requires attention. Using the rearview mirror and the side mirrors, turning one's head to see out the side windows and the back, and checking the car's blind spots are all part of searching out and recognizing potential problems.

In laboratory tests and in a report by the U.S. Department of Transportation, it has been documented that drinking impairs people's ability to divide attention among the tasks necessary to drive safely. Alcohol also slows the rate at which the brain processes information, interfering with its ability to register important messages.

Skills such as concentrating, observing traffic signs, and noticing other things on or near the road all take a backseat when the driver is impaired.

Tracking Skills

Have you ever seen a child manage a steering wheel on a video game? Kids "drive" by yanking the wheel back and forth, to the left, to the right, again and again. If you were in a car with a driver like that, you'd probably feel sick and end up off the road.

Tracking skills involve using the steering wheel in coordination with what you see through the windshield.

To keep the car in your lane or make a turn, you need sharp tracking skills and plenty of practice. Backing up, a related skill, is challenging because your brain needs to register tracking information while your body is turned around. It becomes confusing, and your attention needs to be sharp, especially on wet or icy nights.

Reaction Time

Reaction time, or the time it takes to begin responding to a situation, is crucial in driving. Slamming on your brakes, veering to the side of the road, or scooting into the other lane to avoid a collision requires a quick reaction in addition to the previously mentioned driving skills. Alcohol consumption is known to slow a person's reaction time, and the effect worsens the more one drinks.

PICTURES OF A CRASH-TEST DUMMY

In his book *Drinking and Driving: Know Your Limits and Liabilities,* Dr. Marshall B. Stearn discusses an eye-opening demonstration.

One Memorial Day weekend, the Madigan Army Hospital in Tacoma, Washington, documented the effects of a high-speed car crash. To promote a safety campaign, it sent a mannequin in a car moving at 55 miles (88.5 kilometers) per hour crashing into a tree. With time-lapse photography, the following graphic sequence of events was captured:

- **One-tenth of a second after impact:** The front bumper and chrome frosting of the grillwork collapse. Slivers of steel penetrate the tree to a depth of more than 1 inch (2.5 centimeters).

- **Two-tenths of a second after impact:** The hood crumples and smashes into the windshield. Spinning rear wheels leave the ground. As the fender comes into contact with the tree, the car bends in the middle, with the rear end buckling over the front end.

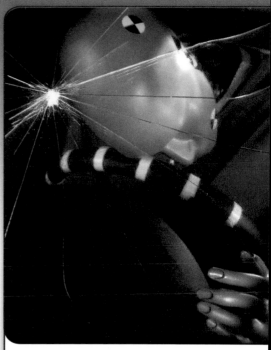

A mannequin traveling in a car at 55 miles per hour (88.5 km/h) crashes, illustrating the devastating effects of a collision within the first second after the impact.

- **Three-tenths of a second after impact:** The mannequin's body is now off the seat, upright, knees pressing against the dashboard. The plastic and steel frame of the steering wheel begins to bend under the weight of the mannequin. Its head is near the sun visor, the chest above the steering column.

- **Four-tenths of a second after impact:** The car's front 24 inches (61 cm) have been demolished, but the rear end is still traveling at an estimated 35 miles (56 km) per hour. The mannequin is still traveling at 55 miles (88.5 km) per hour. The heavy engine block crunches into the tree. The rear end of the car, still bucking like a horse, rises high enough to scrape bark off low branches.

- **Five-tenths of a second after impact:** The mannequin's hands, frozen onto the steering wheel, bend the steering column into an almost vertical position. The force of gravity then pushes its body into the steering column.

- **Six-tenths of a second after impact:** The brake pedal shears off at the floorboard. The chassis bends in the middle, shearing body bolts. The rear of the car begins to fall back down; its spinning wheels dig into the ground.

- **Seven-tenths of a second after impact:** The seat of the car rams forward, pinning the mannequin against the steering shaft; the hinges tear, and the doors spring open.

Close your eyes and see yourself as the driver or passenger of this car. It doesn't take much imagination to conjure up the ghastly picture of what happens to the people inside. Even if you were the best driver in the world, it would be almost impossible to respond quickly enough to such an emergency: seven-tenths of a second pass and it is over. Even if an air bag inflated, imagine the force of the impact if the car were traveling faster, perhaps 70 miles (113 km) or 75 miles (121 km) per hour. Add to this scenario the effect of alcohol on the driver. Making immediate and appropriate judgments in trying to avoid this tragic event would not be possible.

"I'm OK to drive" is the oft-repeated statement when a party is breaking up. Believing that your driving skills are as good when you are drinking as they are when you are sober is a common effect of alcohol. In several studies, drivers knocked over orange cones and ran down flags, but they still believed they drove as well as they did when not drunk. To drive safely and minimize the risks of getting in a motor vehicle crash, you need to be sharp, alert, and in control. Drinking interferes with your emotions, your brain, your coordination, and all of the skills necessary to drive safely.

CHAPTER 3

THE SOCIAL AND EMOTIONAL ASPECTS OF DRINKING AND DRIVING

The teen years are a time for separating from your parents and establishing your own identity. Driving a car is one of the steps toward freedom and taking control of your own life. Along with this freedom comes the responsibility of making healthy decisions. Knowing the facts about drinking, as well as strengthening your skills in dealing with others, will help you make the right choices.

WHY DO TEENS DRINK?

We have already discussed peer pressure as one reason why teens drink. However, peer pressure is not the only reason. Some people point to the media as an influence on teen drinking. Television, movies, Web sites, and ads make drinking look like a fun way to socialize and meet people to date. Characters in movies, books, and TV shows often turn to alcohol for a good time or to help them relax. Teens may also observe their parents and other adults enjoying alcohol.

For some teens, being "in" with their circle of friends means drinking. Other teens are attracted to alcohol because it is illegal; drinking is a way for them to rebel. Teens drink for other reasons, too, including:

Teens may choose to drink for many reasons, including peer pressure, boredom, anxiety, anger, or curiosity. Seeing TV characters drinking alcohol, as they do on shows like *Jersey Shore*, may also have an influence.

- Tension or anxiety ("I had a tough day. I need a drink.")
- Alienation or loneliness ("I don't have anybody to hang out with. Who wants to be with a loser like me?")
- Boredom ("What else is there to do around here?")
- Disappointment and bitterness ("There she is with her new boyfriend. I can't believe she dumped me to go out with that jerk.")
- Sadness ("Life stinks.")

- Anger ("I am so sick of my parents criticizing everything I do.")
- Enjoyment ("I like to drink. It's fun.")
- Experimentation ("It's just something I'm trying out. I can handle it.")
- Emotional turmoil ("My parents just went through the worst divorce. Drinking helps block out my reality right now.")
- Peer pressure ("I can drink you under the table any day. Watch me.")

Some young people start drinking to help them lose their inhibitions and deal with social anxiety. Alcohol can give a person a temporary—and false—sense of confidence. As the person continues to drink, the decision-making part of the brain gets muddled, and he or she may make poor decisions or no decisions at all. Serious and dangerous consequences often result.

TEENS AND ALCOHOLISM

Alcohol is the most widely used drug. In the United States, the average age at which young people begin to drink is around fourteen, according to the National Institute on Alcohol Abuse and Alcoholism (NIAAA). Does this surprise you? Many young drinkers hide the fact that they drink. They may steal their liquor from home or get an adult to buy it for them. They drink alone in their rooms and camouflage the evidence with breath mints and eyedrops.

Research shows that if a person begins drinking at an early age, he or she is more likely to be a heavy drinker in the teen years and as an adult. How your parents drink also influences your drinking habits. In fact, most kids have their first drink at home. Unfortunately, alcoholism—the disease of being physically and psychologically dependent on alcohol—develops more quickly and with less alcohol for teens than for adults. A young person can become an alcoholic in one or two years. If a person drinks alcohol on a regular basis or as a means to escape problems and relieve stress, he or she may have a drinking problem. This could lead to alcohol dependence (addiction).

Alcoholism develops more quickly—and with less alcohol—in teens than it does in adults.

You may have heard of something called tolerance. Tolerance means with frequent drinking over time, the brain can change its sensitivity to alcohol and "tolerate" higher levels. As a result, the person needs to drink more alcohol to feel any of its effects. Developing tolerance can be a symptom of alcohol dependence.

ARE SOME DRINKS MORE ADDICTIVE THAN OTHERS?

It is important to be aware that beer and wine are just as intoxicating—and just as addictive—as hard liquors such as whiskey, vodka, and rum. Many teens and adults believe that because beer and wine contain less alcohol than hard liquor, they are less dangerous. It is true that the average beer (about 5 percent alcohol), table wine (about 12 percent alcohol), and hard liquor (about 40 percent alcohol) do vary in alcohol content. However, it is really the amount that you drink of each that matters. One 12-ounce (355-milliliter) can of beer, one 5-ounce (148-mL) glass of wine, and one 1.5-ounce (30-mL) shot of liquor all contain the same amount of alcohol. Without realizing it, you could be considered a problem drinker just by drinking a few beers a day.

Another common misperception, which is probably due to their sweet taste, is that wine coolers, alcopops, and malt liquor beverages contain less alcohol. In reality, these drinks contain approximately 5.5 percent alcohol—as much as beer. The fruity taste is very appealing to young people who are beginning to experiment with alcohol. But even though they seem harmless, these beverages still act as a depressant, impair your judgment, and can lead to alcohol dependence.

HOW MANY TEENS DRINK?

"Monitoring the Future" is a yearly survey of alcohol and drug use among more than 46,000 eighth, tenth, and twelfth graders all over the country. It has been conducted every year since 1975 by the Institute for Social Research at the University of Michigan, Ann Arbor, and is funded by the National Institute on Drug Abuse.

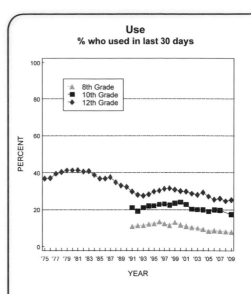

Use
% who used in last 30 days

The proportions of eighth, tenth, and twelfth graders who admitted drinking an alcoholic beverage in the past month were 15, 30, and 44 percent, respectively, according to the 2009 "Monitoring the Future" survey.

Participants in the survey reveal information about their use of drugs and alcohol. The data is organized into the categories of Lifetime Use, Yearly Use, Monthly Use, and Daily Use. Also included is information about binge drinking (consuming five or more drinks in a row in the past two weeks).

According to the 2009 survey results, there has been a steady decline in the percentage of seniors who have reported drinking at all during their teen years (from 68.8 percent in 1999 to 54.6 percent in 2009). Alcohol, however, remains one of the top drugs used among teens.

Even though teen drinking may be decreasing, the numbers from the survey are still disturbing. The statistics show that among twelfth graders in 2009, more than 40 percent admitted to drinking during the past month. More than 25 percent said they became drunk during that time. Almost 3 percent of twelfth graders reported daily use of alcohol. The survey also found that more than 25.2 percent of twelfth graders have engaged in binge drinking at least once.

Alcohol and drug use was noted among younger teens as well. Nearly 15 percent of eighth graders and close to 30 percent of tenth graders reported drinking alcohol within the last thirty days when the survey was taken in 2009.

You Decide: Drinking and Driving Scenarios

You never know when the time will come for you to make a decision about drinking and driving. It isn't easy to decide on a responsible course of action when you are under pressure from others, especially your friends. Situations can unfold quickly, leaving you with only a brief time to weigh the consequences of your actions. You may never have been in such a pressured situation before. Further, you may have no past experience that would help you make the right decision. An impulsive choice is rarely the best one. It is better to think about how you will act *before* you are in a high-pressure situation.

Here are some hypothetical situations in which you may find yourself someday. Think about them to give yourself some practice in decision making. Sort through the questions to test out your skills. There is no one answer that will work in every situation. A lot is left up to you, just as it is in real life.

Party Girls

Melissa and her friend Kasey drove to a party on a Friday night. The party was at their friend Tim's house. Tim's parents were out of town. His house was in another suburb about half an hour's drive from the girls' neighborhood.

Melissa and Kasey usually picked a designated driver, but that night they forgot. Melissa assumed that since Kasey drove them there, she would also drive them home and therefore wouldn't drink. Kasey, on the other hand, assumed that since she had driven to the party, Melissa would drive them home. Because both girls thought the other would drive, they both had some drinks at the party. It was only when the party was winding down and they went out to the car that they realized they both had been drinking. Walking home was out of the question. What should they do?

- How could Melissa and Kasey have avoided this situation?
- What can they do now to get a safe ride home?
- When you go out with friends and think you may drink that night, do you designate a driver who will not drink?

Which statement best describes what you would do if you were in Melissa and Kasey's situation?

- "I would ask Tim if we could crash there for the night."
- "I would see who drank less, and that person would drive home."
- "I would call my parents and tell them the truth that we'd both been drinking. I would ask them to pick us up."
- "I would call my parents and tell them we were having car trouble so that they'd come and get us."
- "I would ask a sober person at the party to drive us home."

Melissa and Kasey's scenario demonstrates the importance of having a plan to designate a non-drinking driver, as well as sticking to that plan every time you go out. Forgetting to designate a driver, even just one time, can put you at risk for driving drunk or riding with a drunk driver. Better yet, avoiding drinking altogether will improve your chances of staying safe.

It's also important to develop a plan with your parents in case you get into this type of situation. We will discuss such plans in a later chapter.

Cute but Deadly

Nicole met Doug when she was working at the mall. He had graduated from high school a few years before and was a manager at one of the stores. Nicole was nervous about dating someone older, but she was excited, too.

One night Doug stopped by the cafe where Nicole worked and said, "I'm having some people over tonight.

I'd really like you to come, too." He gave Nicole his address. That night, she drove over to his apartment. A bunch of his friends were there, drinking wine and beer. Nicole felt uncomfortable showing up alone at a party where she didn't know anyone but Doug. She decided to have one glass of wine so that she would relax. After a while, it was fun to sit on the couch with a glass of wine and have Doug's arm around her. After a few more glasses of wine, she felt a little dizzy and groggy. Nicole noticed that it was past her curfew.

Her legs were wobbly, and she realized that she was really drunk. Nobody else at the party looked like they were in any shape to drive either.

- How could Nicole have avoided her situation?
- What can Nicole do now to get home safely?
- Have you ever been in a situation where you planned to drink just a little and ended up drinking too much?

Again, Nicole's situation shows the importance of planning ahead. If you are the only person driving, you are the designated driver, and even a little alcohol is too much. As Nicole found out, one drink can lead to another and another. Decide from the start that you will not even have one.

Before you go somewhere, determine whether alcohol will be involved. Assess the safety of the situation in general. Will you be with people you know well? Does someone know where you are? It's often a good idea to bring along a friend. Stay aware of your surroundings and the people around you.

Twisted Sister

Chuck and his friends were waiting in front of the movie theater. Dave's sister Chloe was going to pick them up after the movie. All of a sudden, her car came screeching into the parking lot. Chuck noticed beer cans in the back seat of the car. Chloe's boyfriend, who sat in the passenger seat, was drinking from a beer can concealed in a paper bag. Chuck was pretty sure from the way Chloe was acting that she had been drinking, too. His friends Dave and Zack piled into the car, but Chuck hung back. He didn't feel safe getting into the car. "Hey, get in!" Dave said. "What are you waiting for?"

- If you were Chuck, what would you say to Dave?
- Would you ask Chloe if she had been drinking?
- Would you get into the car?
- What are Chuck's other options for getting home?

It can be hard to confront a driver you think has been drinking. Many times, drunk drivers are defensive. They don't want to admit that they shouldn't be driving. The alcohol may make them more resistant than usual. If the person you think is driving drunk is older than you, it can be even more difficult to confront him or her. But lives could be at stake, so it is important to do your best to keep a drunk person from driving.

If your friends don't seem to be worried, it can be hard to be the one to speak up. They may accuse you of being paranoid. But if you feel there is real danger involved, trust your instincts.

Abusive Date

Katie was on her first date with Brian. They planned to go to a party and then to a late movie. On the way to the movie, Katie noticed that Brian was veering into the other lane. She remembered that he had been drinking at the party. She asked him to pull over. When they stopped, Brian leaned over and started kissing her. He grabbed her and tugged at the buttons of her clothing. Katie was angry and scared. She told him to stop, but he wouldn't. Finally, Katie pushed him away and got out of the car. Brian was angry and sped away.

- How will Katie get home?
- Could Katie have done something to avoid this situation?
- Katie knows that Brian is driving drunk. Should she call his parents? The police?

Sometimes, you may think someone is in decent shape to drive, and you get in the car. But what if you realize too late that the driver is not OK? And what if he or she pushes you to do something you don't want to do?

Try not to take rides from people unless they are your designated driver or you know for sure that they have not been drinking. Plan ahead so that you aren't in a situation where you have no choice but to ride with someone you don't know well. If you are going someplace where alcohol may be served, you must discuss who will do the driving, even if it's hard to bring up the topic. A little awkwardness now is better than a car crash later.

Making decisions like the ones presented above can be tied to your feelings about yourself. If you believe in yourself, that will influence your choices. But if your self-esteem is low, you may be easily influenced by others and let them make decisions for you, decisions that may not be in your best interest.

REFUSAL SKILLS

Your peers have a strong influence on the choices you make. However, you can also have an influence on others. Working on your refusal skills can help you have more control in situations related to drinking and driving.

The ideas below are taken from a youth character-building program started by Leah Davies of Bend, Oregon. She has trained many parents, school counselors, and teachers through her Kelly Bear Character and Resiliency Education Skills Program. The program suggests eight different ways to say "No" when someone is encouraging you to do something risky:

- **Say "No" or "No, thanks," over and over if necessary.**
  Tell the person, "No, thanks. I don't drink," or "No, I'm the designated driver tonight."

- **Call it what it is.**

  "That's using drugs, and I don't do that."

  "That's against the law for us, and I don't want to get in trouble."

- **Talk about something else.**

  Change the subject: "That was a great game!"

  "Have you finished that project yet?"

- **Ask questions.**

  Turn it back to the peer: "Why do you care if I drink or not?"

  "Why would you want me to drink and drive?"

- **Give reasons.**

  "I don't want to risk losing my license or getting into a crash."

  "My parents would never trust me with the car again."

- **Use humor or sarcasm.**

  "Are you kidding? Beer can really mess up my buff body."

  "Sure, that's all I need to do. I'd be grounded for a month!"

- **Suggest doing something else.**

  "Let's call my mom. She'll pick us up no matter what time it is."

  "How about leaving this party now?"

  "Let's do something else that doesn't involve drinking."

- **If you want their friendship, keep the door open.**

  "If you decide to do something that doesn't involve alcohol, let me know."

You may want to practice these steps as a way to prepare for situations like the ones described in this chapter. Formulate answers that you can use in a drinking-and-driving situation that calls for quick, responsible thinking.

Practice what to say out loud to a friend or in front of a mirror. This will help you feel confident when you have to use these steps to stand up to someone who is trying to influence you to do something dangerous or illegal. These refusal skills will give you a handle on turning peer pressure to your advantage. They will help keep you safe and alive.

INTERVENTION SKILLS

You can also make a difference by stopping someone from driving drunk. NHTSA ran a campaign called "Get the Keys: How You Can Intervene," and offered the following suggestions:

- If the person is a close friend, try a soft, calm approach at first. Suggest that he or she has had too much to drink and it would be better if someone else drove or if he or she took a cab.
- Be calm. Joke about it. Make light of it.
- Try to make it sound like you are doing the person a favor.

By practicing refusal and intervention skills, you can prevent yourself and others from getting behind the wheel after drinking alcohol.

- If it is someone you don't know very well, speak to the person's friends. Have a friend try to persuade him or her to hand over the keys. Usually, he or she will listen.

- If it is a good friend or significant other, tell the person that if he or she insists on driving, you are not going with him or her. Say that you will call someone else for a ride, take a cab, or walk.

- Locate the keys while he or she is preoccupied and take them away. Most likely, he or she will think they're lost and will be forced to find another mode of transportation.

- If possible, avoid embarrassing the person or being confrontational, particularly when dealing with a man.

Keep in mind the campaign's motto: "Friends don't let friends drive drunk." You can make the difference between a person getting home safe and taking the risk of driving drunk.

MYTH

Everyone drinks.

FACT

Not as many teens drink as you may think. Only about 14.7 percent of young people ages twelve to seventeen reported drinking during the last thirty days, according to the 2009 National Survey on Drug Use and Health from the Substance Abuse and Mental Health Services Administration (SAMHSA). That means that 85.3 percent of twelve- to seventeen-year-olds did not drink during the month prior to the survey.

MYTH

Just like the saying goes, "Beer before liquor, never sicker. Liquor before beer, in the clear."

FACT

Your BAC determines your level of intoxication. It doesn't matter what type of alcohol you choose to consume. A drink is a drink, and too much of any combination can make you sick.

MYTH

Sobriety checkpoints are easy for drunk drivers to avoid. They can just turn around and take a detour or switch drivers beforehand.

FACT

Most well-run checkpoints include a police officer stationed down the road to observe such behavior. If drivers make a U-turn to avoid them, the police can follow the vehicle for a short distance to observe its operation and make a decision to pull the vehicle over.

MYTHS AND FACTS

CHAPTER 4

DRINKING AND DRIVING LAWS

Are you a gambler? How often do you think you can beat the odds? Every time you drink and drive, or get into a car with an intoxicated driver, you are pushing your luck. Maybe you made it home safely the last time, just grazing the tires of your parents' car along the curb. You woke up in your own bed. The car was parked in the driveway. No big deal, right?

What about the next time? Or the next? How long do you think someone can beat the odds before his or her luck runs out?

Driving after drinking is one of the biggest gambles you can take with your life and the lives of others. A high percentage of fatal crashes happen because a driver is intoxicated. The more one attempts to beat the odds, the more likely a crash, an arrest, or death will occur.

UNDERAGE DRINKING LAWS

There has been a strong push to crack down on and prevent underage drinking. The first step in reducing drinking and driving among teens is to reduce teen drinking. According to the Centers for Disease Control and Prevention's (CDC) Youth Risk Behavior Surveillance Survey, in 2009 an estimated 42 percent of teens obtained alcohol from someone else, such as a parent, sibling, acquaintance, or stranger. Other teens have been able to obtain alcohol through the use of fake IDs or by purchasing the liquor themselves without being properly carded. However, fewer teens are obtaining alcohol in this manner today than in the past. This is partly due to stricter laws, heavier fines, and undercover programs designed to catch business owners in the act of selling alcohol to teens.

One successful program in Delaware, called the Cooperative Underage Witness Program, aims to crack down on establishments that cater to the

This ad is one of the many campaign tools available for download from NHTSA's Web site (http://www.stopimpaireddriving.org).

underage drinking crowd. Volunteers who are between sixteen and twenty years old order drinks in bars that are known to have served minors in the past and that are sources of complaint in the community. The volunteer is given a Breathalyzer test before and after going into the bar. If he or she is served alcohol, the establishment can be charged with serving a minor.

Stiffer penalties continue to crop up across the country to address this problem. Several states have enacted laws for accomplices to underage drinking. Persons twenty-one years of age or older that purchase alcohol or provide alcohol to underage individuals may be subject to:

- Fines of up to $2,000
- A misdemeanor charge of contributing to the delinquency of a minor
- Retail license suspension
- Possible jail time/probation

Persons twenty-one years or older that let a minor use their identification for the purpose of buying alcoholic beverages can face the above consequences, plus:

- Fines up to $1,000
- Arrest
- Up to six months of imprisonment

States continue to move in the direction of tougher penalties for underage drinkers. States hope the stronger laws will deter young people from drinking and driving. They are also designed to provide early detection and treatment for those who show a tendency toward alcohol abuse.

SOCIAL HOST LIABILITY LAWS

Some teens may ask, "What about drinking at your own or someone else's house? My parents say they would

Adults that purchase alcohol for minors and/or allow them to party on their property can face heavy consequences under social host liability laws.

rather know where, what, and with whom I'm drinking. So they let us stay at my house and drink."

Social host liability laws make this kind of activity illegal. Charges can be filed against property owners, parents, or guardians that allow underage use of alcohol or drugs on the premises. If minors are drinking on private property and the owner, parents, or guardians are present, they can be arrested and charged with allowing underage drinking, as well as creating and maintaining a condition that endangers the safety and health of individuals.

Even if the drinking occurs when the owners, parents, or guardians are not present, they can still be held liable. Often, teens plan a party when someone's parents are not at home. The police may break up the party, but by then damage may have occurred to the house, property, or people. The parents may have to spend money to repair the damages or compensate other parents for what happened to their kids at the party. They may also face civil or criminal fines, imprisonment, and the threat of being sued for emotional pain and suffering.

Imagine this scenario: you have a party at a friend's house. It gets a little wild toward the end. Two guys get into a fight, and one of them gets his front teeth knocked out. There are broken beer bottles and blood all over the rug and furniture in the living room. The parents of the injured person threaten to sue your friend's parents, who didn't even know about the party, for negligence.

If alcohol is served in a home, the adults (anyone over twenty-one) may be held liable for any person who is injured as a result of underage drinking in their home, in their vehicles, or on their property. Involvement in such an activity could lead to the loss of a home or other assets, business, jail time, and fines.

Stiffer penalties for underage drinking aim to keep teens alcohol-free. A person who hasn't had any alcohol is less likely to be a danger to others on the road.

ZERO TOLERANCE LAWS

It is illegal in every state for people under the age of twenty-one to buy, possess, drink, or transport open alcoholic beverages. Through zero tolerance laws, states have made it illegal for persons under twenty-one to drink at all and then drive. These laws penalize youths for operating a vehicle with any trace of alcohol in their systems. Depending on the state, even a negligible level, such as .01 or .02, may be penalized.

If police officers have probable cause to believe that drivers have been drinking, the zero tolerance law allows them to give breath tests to those under twenty-one. If a driver refuses the test, or if the test shows any level of alcohol in the blood, the driver faces the following consequences:

- Fines up to $1,000
- Mandatory loss of driving privileges for six months to a year
- Community service
- Participation in an alcohol education and highway safety program
- Additional penalties as imposed by the judge

If a person is not driving but is caught drinking while underage, some of the same penalties might apply. One can temporarily lose driving privileges, even if no car is involved. For those who do not yet have a driver's license, the suspension starts when they are eligible.

More license suspension time can be added if a person is drinking while in a motor vehicle, even if he or she is not the driver. If caught, a person can be required to successfully complete an alcohol rehabilitation program.

NHTSA reports that in 2008, 31 percent of fifteen to twenty year olds who were killed in crashes had a BAC of .01 or higher. Twenty-five percent had a BAC of .08 or higher. Strict enforcement of zero tolerance laws can prevent many fatal crashes every year. These zero tolerance laws support existing state laws that forbid the sale and serving of alcohol to underage drinkers. Keeping teens alive is the main reason for these new, stricter laws.

.08 BAC PER SE LAWS

A per se law means that for those over twenty-one, it is illegal in and of itself to drive with an alcohol concentration at or above a certain level. It does not matter if the person shows other signs of intoxication (slurred speech, erratic driving, or loss of balance, for example). Alcohol concentration is based on either the number of grams of alcohol in 100 milliliters (3.38 ounces) of blood or the number of grams of alcohol in 210 liters (7,101 oz) of breath.

As of August 2005, all states had adopted an illegal per se law at the .08 BAC level. These laws make it

An ignition interlock system forces the driver to blow into a device that tests BAC in order to start the car. This kind of system is a requirement in twelve states for convicted DUI offenders.

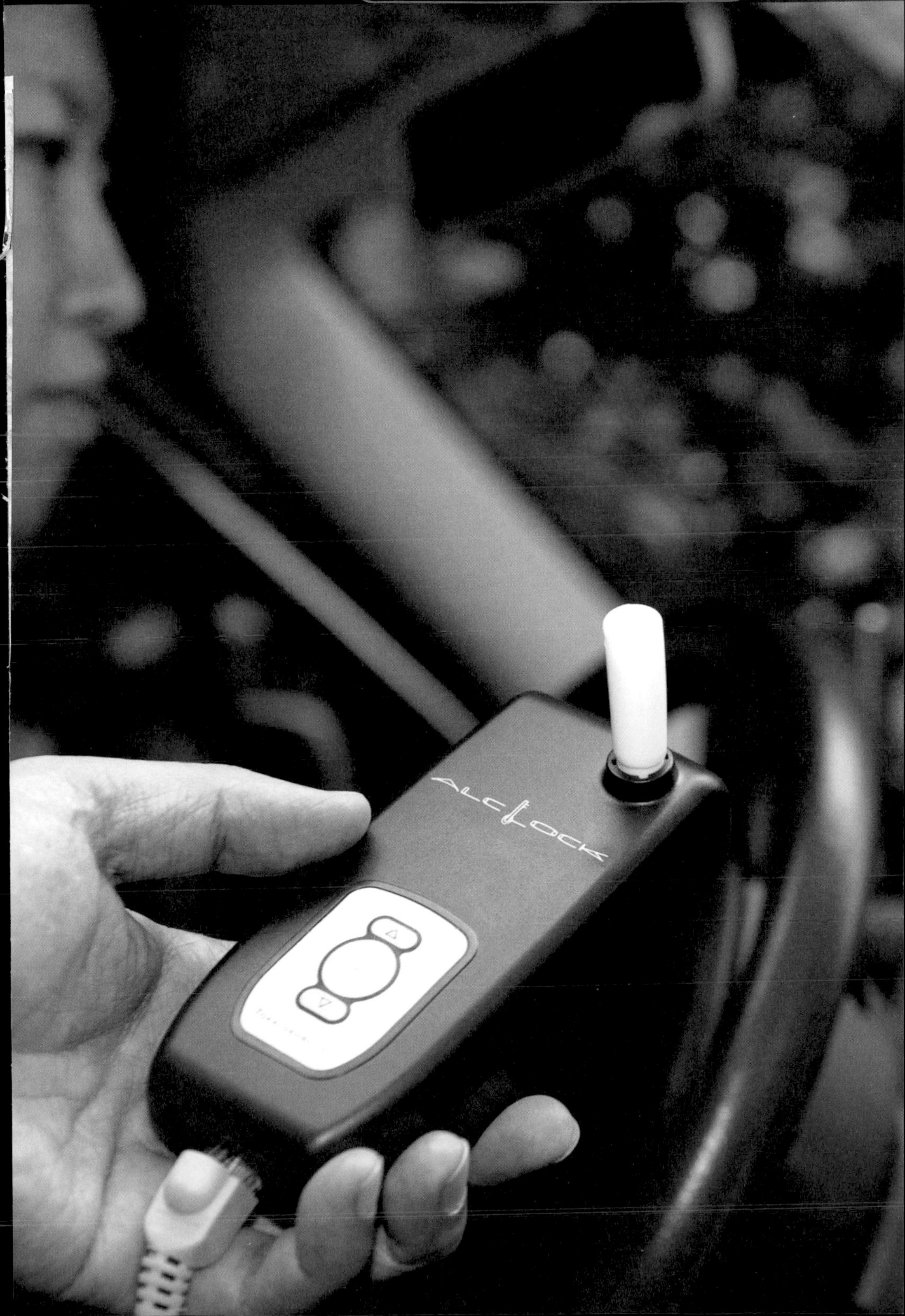
ALCOLOCK

illegal to drive or be in control of a motor vehicle with a BAC of .08 or higher.

Research indicates that even at low blood alcohol levels, many drivers are impaired and present a danger to themselves and to others. Tolerance varies from person to person. Some drivers have problems driving even at .02 BAC levels. At .08, even experienced drivers are affected. Studies by NHTSA and other agencies show that .08 BAC laws reduce alcohol-related crashes and fatalities. Data collected in California shows that lowering the legal limit from .10 to .08 BAC contributed to a 12 percent reduction in deaths due to DUI in the first year after the law went into effect.

In addition, twelve states (Alaska, Arizona, Arkansas, Colorado, Hawaii, Illinois, Louisiana, Nebraska, New Mexico, New York, Utah, and Washington) have used ignition interlocks for convicted DUI offenders, even on the first offense. Ignition interlocks are a system whereby the offender blows into a device that can detect the BAC. The car cannot be started if the person's BAC is above a certain level (usually .02 to .04). Meeting NHTSA standards requires an additional breath test to occur while driving. Lastly, forty-two states, the District of Columbia, and Guam have increased penalties for a high BAC.

ADMINISTRATIVE LICENSE REVOCATION

In order to give drivers an extra incentive to follow the law, many states have instituted new policies regarding driver's licenses. With these new policies, drivers risk losing their licenses if they violate laws regarding drinking and driving.

Administrative license revocation, or ALR, allows an arresting officer to immediately confiscate the license of any driver who is found with a BAC at or above the legal limit, or who refuses to take a BAC test. A temporary driving permit is given for a short time, such as two or three weeks, and then the driver is notified of his or her right to appeal the revocation. If there is no appeal, or if the revocation is upheld, the offender loses the right to drive for a set period of time (ninety days for a first offense in most states and longer for subsequent offenses). Governors Highway Safety Association (GHSA) reports that as of September 2010, ALR laws had been passed in forty-three states, the District of Columbia, the Northern Mariana Islands, and the Virgin Islands.

In states without ALR laws, drunk drivers might not lose their licenses until they are convicted in criminal court. There may be a considerable amount of time between the drunk-driving incident and the date when the license is actually revoked. If a plea bargain is reached (admitting to a lesser offense than the one charged), the offender's license may not be revoked at all.

ALR laws are effective because they immediately punish the drunk driver for breaking the law. They are also a deterrent. Drivers who are arrested and have their licenses revoked under ALR laws are less likely to drink and drive again. People who have not been arrested are also discouraged from drinking and driving because they

Drivers who are suspected of drunk driving can be pulled over by a police officer and asked to perform a variety of field sobriety tests.

know they can lose their license immediately if they are caught.

CONSEQUENCES OF DRINKING AND DRIVING

Unfortunately, despite efforts to prevent people from drinking and driving, many make the mistake of doing it anyway. The consequences of this mistake are serious. The following are typical repercussions of driving under the influence of alcohol.

Arrest for DUI

Being arrested for DUI (driving under the influence) is serious business. It's expensive, too. Lawyer's fees, fines, and time in jail are the results of being convicted of DUI. You may also have heard of DWI (driving while intoxicated). DUI and DWI are used interchangeably, depending on the state.

With the strong push to keep intoxicated drivers off America's roads, most towns have strengthened the enforcement of drunk-driving laws. During holiday weekends and other busy times, checkpoints are set up. Drivers are stopped at random to determine if they have been drinking. Police also pull over suspicious drivers at any time of the year.

Drivers pulled over on suspicion of drinking and driving are asked to take a field sobriety test (e.g., walking a straight line, saying the alphabet) and/or breath test to assess the alcohol concentration in the body. If a person fails the test or refuses to take it, his or her driver's license can be automatically revoked, even before going to court.

"Wait a minute, that's not fair!" you might say. "Isn't that 'guilty until proven innocent' instead of the other way around?"

Due to the severity of the drunk-driving laws, a driver *must* take the tests to prove his or her innocence. Some may see this as an example of losing freedom. However, when a person gets behind the wheel of a potentially lethal weapon while intoxicated, that person is denying others their freedom to ride in safety.

Conviction and Sentencing

A person who is arrested for drunk driving must appear in court. The judge decides the sentence. A DUI conviction makes a person a lawbreaker, a criminal. A person who is convicted has to face the consequences, which can include the following legal penalties, according to the Insurance Institute for Highway Safety (IIHS):

- **Fines.** Each state has specific laws. For DUI, offenders can expect to pay various fines for a first conviction.

- **Jail.** Spending anywhere from forty-eight hours to a year in jail is a penalty for a first-time DUI. Some states allow offenders to do community service instead of jail time by working in their town or community rebuilding, cleaning up, or helping others.

- **Probation.** Instead of jail time, a few states may place offenders on probation. This means that the person's behavior and lifestyle are monitored for a period of time, possibly one to three years. The probation officer may check with the person's family, school, and employer to make sure he or she is staying out of trouble. The offender must report to the probation officer once a month or at appointed times.

- **Rehabilitation.** Most DUI laws require offenders to complete a driver improvement program. Many states also require offenders to undergo an alcohol rehabilitation program to help them recognize and deal with their drinking problem.

- **License revocation.** A person convicted of DUI will lose his or her license for at least several months, perhaps as long as a year.

Financial and Personal Problems

Being arrested for drunk driving can cause financial and personal difficulties. For example, you might need to hire a lawyer to help you fight a DUI arrest. Add to that expense the fine you will have to pay if you are convicted. You will probably find that you don't have enough money to cover the costs.

In addition, your auto insurance premium will inevitably rise. Insurance companies do not like risky drivers because chances are high that such drivers will cost them a lot of money. Since by law you must insure your vehicle, an alcohol-related conviction can cost you for many years to come.

A DUI conviction can lead to job loss, too. Employers cannot rely on you if you are not able to get to work, whether it is a part-time job after school or full-time employment. License revocation can mean a quick end to your job, especially one in which you are required to drive.

Being arrested and convicted of DUI will not be pleasant for your family either. The worry, stress, and anxiety that you, your parents, and other family members will experience in this situation may be overwhelming. Arguments, accusations, and denials are possible outcomes. Many newspapers report the names of those convicted of DUI. The reactions of people in your community are hard to predict, but chances are they won't be positive.

The consequences of DUI outlined above are for first-time offenders. According to Mothers Against Drunk Driving (MADD), the average total cost for a first-time offender can range from $7,828 to $10,828! Things get more serious if you are convicted a second time within a certain number of years. A third conviction increases jail time and fines.

It's a different story if you are convicted of DUI and have caused injury or death to another person. People convicted in these circumstances can spend years in prison, pay heavy fines, and lose their licenses for quite a few years. There are also serious emotional consequences, including feelings of guilt for having hurt or killed another person.

The laws in each state may vary. Laws may also change often. Check with your local police department or state department of motor vehicles for your state's laws.

INTERVENTION AND REHABILITATION PROGRAMS

A drunk-driving incident indicates that the driver has a problem with alcohol. He or she may even be an alcoholic. This situation is sometimes addressed by making alcoholism treatment a part of the punishment for drunk driving.

ASK DR. JAN, PSYCHOLOGIST

First name: Sean

Question:
My father drinks a lot at home, and I think he would be considered an alcoholic. Sometimes, he drives under the influence of alcohol, even though he knows it is against the law. How can I get him to stop?

Answer:
Unfortunately, alcohol is one of the most addictive drugs on the planet. If your dad is an alcoholic, he may need to get help in order to address his drinking. As with many addictions, it can be very difficult at first to get the substance abuser to acknowledge that he has a problem and then participate in treatment. You should also know that the chances that a child will become an alcoholic increase if a parent suffers from alcoholism. So, if you are correct about your dad, you and your siblings would be wise to avoid drinking alcohol altogether.

In response to your question, you cannot get your dad to stop drinking unless he is willing to try to change his behavior. What you can do is let him know that you love him and are concerned for his safety and the safety of your family members when he drives under the influence of alcohol. If that would be too difficult, it might be best to first have the conversation with your mom about the best way to approach your dad about his drinking. If that is not possible, it may be helpful to speak to a trusted adult (e.g. school staff, a relative, or a family friend).

Sometimes, families will organize an intervention: they plan a meeting with a group of family members and friends to confront the substance abuser with their concerns if they have already tried in vain to talk to him or her individually. It is often useful to have a mental health professional with expertise in addiction issues present to help lead the intervention.

If all of this fails, families then have to take the difficult step of getting the police involved. Once a driver gets arrested for driving while intoxicated, the courts often mandate substance abuse treatment. While these steps are very difficult, it would be far worse for your dad, a family member, or an innocent bystander to get hurt or killed before something is done about it. I would also encourage you (and your family) to refuse to get in the car if your dad has been drinking.

Ask a Question

Do you have a question that you would like answered? E-mail your question to Dr. Jan at drjan@rosenpub.com. If your question is selected, it will appear on the Teen Health & Wellness Web site in "Dr. Jan's Corner."

If you have an urgent question on a health or wellness issue, we strongly encourage you to call a hotline to speak to a qualified professional or speak to a trusted adult, such as a parent, teacher, or guidance counselor. You can find hotlines listed in the For More Information section of this book, or at www.teenhealthandwellness.com/static/hotlines.

Alcohol rehabilitation programs usually involve taking the DUI offender to a treatment center to deal with the drinking problem. These programs are not just an easy way out of jail time or a fine. They usually are required in addition to other penalties, not in place of them. Offenders still have to pay the court-imposed fines, and they have to pay for the program itself. In many cases, follow-up probation may require that offenders attend Alcoholics Anonymous (AA) meetings or that they are monitored by other social agencies.

The first step of rehab, which is also the hardest step, is for someone to admit that he or she has a problem. Having a problem doesn't mean that you drink every day or even every weekend. But if alcohol plays an important part in your life, and you drink to deal with life's ups and downs, a rehab program can help you redirect your life.

Intervention programs, such as retraining and rehab, are fairly successful, especially for younger DUI offenders. The young offender has had fewer years in which to become a heavy drinker. He or she is also more physically stable. A young person can be more open to intervention and the chance to redirect his or her life. Intervention programs are designed to get help for those already in trouble and reduce the chances of repeat DUI crimes. Unfortunately, NHTSA estimates that first-time offenders account for half to two-thirds of the continuing drunk-driving problem.

Other laws pertaining to drunk driving are also becoming stricter. For example, drunk-driving offenders are not permitted to engage in plea bargaining in some states. This means that offenders cannot plead guilty to a lesser charge instead of the more serious charge for which they were arrested. In many cases, penalties are mandatory. The days of the suspended sentence, at least for DUI offenses, are vanishing. A suspended sentence is one in which the conviction stands but the offender does not have to serve the sentence as long as he or she does not get in trouble again.

In addition, victims of DUI offenders or their families now have a right to make a statement to the judge, known as a victim impact statement, before sentencing in cases involving death or serious injury.

Graduated Driver Licensing Laws

Many young people are involved in collisions and fatal crashes because of immaturity and a lack of driving experience. Newer licensing procedures, called graduated driver licensing laws (GDL), are designed to address these factors. The goal is to expose young drivers to progressively more difficult driving experiences before they get a full license.

In the mid-1990s, the Institute for Highway Safety, National Safety Council, National Transportation Safety Board, and National Highway Traffic Safety Administration collaborated to establish a national GDL model. The model program consists of three stages, each with recommended components and restrictions. They are:

New Jersey is the first state to require young drivers with a graduated license to display decals on their vehicles identifying them as new drivers.

Stage One: Learner's Permit

- Minimum age for a permit is sixteen years old.
- Driver must pass vision test and knowledge test, including rules of the road, signs, and signals.
- A licensed adult (at least twenty-one years of age) must be in the vehicle at all times.
- All people in the car must wear seat belts.
- Zero alcohol is consumed while driving.
- Driver completes basic driver training.
- Driver adheres to teenage passenger restrictions.
- Parental certification of thirty to fifty practice hours.
- No use of portable electronic communication and entertainment devices.

- Permit is visually distinctive from other driver's licenses.
- Driver must remain crash- and conviction-free for six months in order to move on to the next stage.

Stage Two: Intermediate (Provisional) License
- Driver must successfully complete Stage One.
- Minimum age for intermediate license is 16.5 years.
- Driver must pass behind-the-wheel road test.
- All people in the car must wear seat belts.
- Zero alcohol is consumed while driving.
- Nighttime driving restrictions are observed. A licensed adult must be in the vehicle from 10 PM until 5 AM.
- Driver completes advanced driver training.
- Driver improvement actions are initiated at lower point level than for regular drivers.
- Provisional license is visually distinctive from a regular license.
- Teenage passenger restrictions are observed. Car contains no more than one teenage passenger for the first twelve months of the intermediate license. Afterward, the number of teenage passengers is limited to two until age eighteen.
- Driver completes supervised practice.
- No use of portable electronic communication and entertainment devices.
- Must remain crash- and conviction-free for twelve consecutive months in order to move on to the next stage.

Stage Three: Full Licensure
- Driver must successfully complete Stage Two.
- Minimum age for full license is eighteen years in order to lift passenger and night restrictions.
- Zero alcohol is consumed while driving.

GDL laws and components vary from state to state. A September 2010 report from the GHSA shows that all states have three stages, except for North Dakota. The following are some developments highlighted in the report:

- **Restrictions on cell phone use/texting.** Twenty-one states and the District of Columbia restrict cell phone use by novice drivers. Ten states ban texting.
- **Nighttime driving restrictions.** Forty-seven states and the District of Columbia restrict nighttime driving during the intermediate stage.
- **Passenger restrictions.** Forty-four states and the District of Columbia restrict the number of passengers during the intermediate stage.
- **Novice driver decals.** New Jersey is the only state with a measure requiring drivers younger than twenty-one without full-privilege licenses to display decals on their vehicles identifying them as new drivers.

These measures seem to work. According to NHTSA, states such as Florida reported a 9-percent reduction in crashes for drivers ages sixteen and seventeen since instituting a GDL system. Michigan and North Carolina reported a 26- and 25-percent reduction, respectively, in crashes of sixteen-year-olds. Keeping teens alive and driving safely is the goal of stricter licensing laws.

Society is demanding retribution from people who disregard the laws and use their motor vehicle as a potentially lethal weapon because of their drinking and driving. With so many laws on the books and so much information on the topic, people are no longer willing to forgive drunk drivers who say, "I didn't know."

1. What are the drinking-and-driving statistics for my town (e.g., number of teen crashes, under-age drinking violations, etc.)?

2. What are the local laws about drinking and driving? Are there social host liability laws in this area?

3. What resources are available to me in my town?

4. Where can I research more information, and which Web sites can I trust?

5. What advice do you have about resisting peer pressure?

6. What are the current hot topics for my town regarding teen health and safety?

7. Do laws exist for operating other vehicles under the influence, such as boats, ATVs, and bicycles?

8. How does alcohol affect the teen brain?

9. Are sobriety checkpoints and/or seat belt checks done in this community?

10. How can we evaluate our efforts to reduce teen drinking and driving in our school?

10 GREAT QUESTIONS TO ASK A POLICE OFFICER OR PUBLIC SAFETY EXPERT

THE AFTERMATH of DRINKING AND DRIVING

Families and friends who lose someone to a drunk driver must forever cope with the knowledge that their loved one died because of someone else's irresponsible behavior. The following poem was written by an unknown author, but it has frequently circulated as an e-mail forward and in anti-drunk driving Web site resources. There are various adaptations of both the verses and the title, including "I Went to a Party, Mom," "Death of an Innocent," or simply the "Drunk Driving Poem":

I went to a party, Mom,
I remembered what you said.
You told me not to drink, Mom,
So I drank soda instead.

I really felt proud inside, Mom,
The way you said I would.
I didn't drink and drive, Mom,
Even though the others said I should.

I know I did the right thing, Mom,
I know you are always right.
Now the party is finally ending, Mom,
As everyone is driving out of sight.

As I got into my car, Mom,
I knew I'd get home in one piece.
Because of the way you raised me,
So responsible and sweet.

I started to drive away, Mom,
But as I pulled out into the road,
The other car didn't see me, Mom,
And hit me like a load.

As I lay there on the pavement, Mom,
I hear the policeman say,
"The other guy is drunk," Mom,
And now I'm the one who will pay.

I'm lying here dying, Mom...
I wish you'd get here soon.
How could this happen to me, Mom?
My life just burst like a balloon.

There is blood all around me, Mom,
And most of it is mine.
I hear the medic say, Mom,
I'll die in a short time.

I just wanted to tell you, Mom,
I swear I didn't drink.
It was the others, Mom.
The others didn't think.

He was probably at the same party as I.
The only difference is, he drank
And I will die.

Why do people drink, Mom?
It can ruin your whole life.
I'm feeling sharp pains now.
Pains just like a knife.

The guy who hit me is walking, Mom,
And I don't think it's fair.
I'm lying here dying
And all he can do is stare.

Tell my brother not to cry, Mom.
Tell Daddy to be brave.
And when I go to heaven, Mom,
Put "Daddy's Girl" on my grave.

Someone should have told him, Mom,
Not to drink and drive.
If only they had told him, Mom,
I would still be alive.

My breath is getting shorter, Mom.
I'm becoming very scared.
Please don't cry for me, Mom,
When I needed you,
You were always there.

I have one last question, Mom.
Before I say goodbye.
I didn't drink and drive,
So why am I the one to die?

There is no arguing that a fatality caused by a drunk-driving crash can be very tragic. Families are forever altered and lives are shattered. Drunk drivers usually don't think about the hurt they can cause, physically and emotionally, to so many people. Their judgment is impaired, and no one else on the road or on the sidewalk is safe. Although a fatality is truly a tragic event, the fate of some drivers and passengers who survive such a tragedy can be equally devastating. According to the Centers for Disease Control and Prevention (CDC), more than 350,000 drivers ages fifteen to nineteen were injured in motor vehicle crashes in 2009.

SMASHED: TOXIC TALES OF TEENS AND ALCOHOL

In an effort to fight underage drinking and alcohol-related driving, RADD, an organization of the entertainment industry, and coalition members, including HBO Family, the National Organizations for Youth Safety (NOYS), and NHTSA, created a hard-hitting HBO Family documentary and accompanying community toolkit. The documentary is meant to show the real, long-term effects of injury caused by underage drinking and drinking and driving. This TV-14 rated, graphic presentation takes place at the University of Maryland Shock Trauma Center in Baltimore and chronicles real teen crash victims who did not die. Below are synopses of some of the true stories featured in *Smashed*:

- **Timmy, age fifteen:** After drinking a case of beer, Timmy drove his all-terrain vehicle into a tree after swerving to avoid a rabbit. He was not wearing a helmet. We see Timmy rushed into the Shock Trauma Center with severe brain swelling as his parents wait tearfully for him to show signs of cognizance. After a week, he is released into a rehab center, where he must learn to speak and walk again. Five months later, as Timmy celebrates his sixteenth birthday, he is irritable and depressed, and he has begun drinking again. He has recently dropped out of high school and has spent a week in a mandatory detox program.

- **Andy, age nineteen:** Andy was driving home from a friend's house after "a few beers" when his Jeep, going 70 miles (112.6 km) per hour in a 35-mph (56.3-kph) zone, hit an embankment and rolled over four times. Lucky to be alive, Andy is brought into the Shock Trauma Center, where he admits to drinking six to nine beers every day. However, he claims that he is not an alcoholic and that he can control himself. Lying on the emergency room table, his head being stitched together, he agrees to "cut back" on his drinking.

- **Traci, age eighteen:** After "partying" one night, Traci got into a car with a drunk driver, who ended up speeding and slamming into a tree. Traci's head smashed into the windshield, and her brain banged back and forth and twisted inside her skull. She was in a coma for eighty-one days. She also sustained multiple injuries so severe (a ruptured spleen, punctured lung, broken ribs, and smashed pelvis) that she was unable to do anything for herself. Her mother describes her as being "like an infant." Four years later, after painstaking rehabilitation, Traci still struggles with speaking (due to partial paralysis) and spends most of her time at home. About that fateful day, she says, "I just basically ruined my life."

- **Tom, age seventeen:** After drinking a quart of vodka at a local mall, Tom fell twenty feet (six meters) off a landing—and onto a stone floor. Though he denies he's been drinking as he's brought into the Shock Trauma Center, tests confirm that he had consumed alcohol. His family arrives to find him drugged and breathing on a respirator. They wait and pray as doctors remove a dangerous blood clot in his frontal lobe. When Tom's friends come to visit, his mom implores them to change their ways. Since his accident, Tom has been unable to find a job.

- **Katie, age sixteen:** After meeting some guys she didn't know (not realizing that they had been drinking), Katie recalls, "I thought the guy driving was pretty hot, so of course I got in the car with them." She ended up in a crash that left her in a coma for more than seven weeks. She also had a broken arm, a broken leg, and multiple internal injuries. Her mother describes the ensuing struggle to help Katie relearn basic functions, as well as enduring an angry phase (typical of head trauma victims) of lashing out, biting, and hitting. Katie's short-term memory is so impaired that she can not learn properly or even enjoy a movie. She has given up her college plans and is looking for clerical work.

- **Warren, age seventeen:** One day, Warren got a lift home from a friend who had been drinking "a couple" of beers. When the friend's car crashed, Warren's brain, like Traci's, slammed back and forth inside his skull. He now has difficulty sleeping, eating, concentrating, and reading. Warren describes himself as having been "happy-go-lucky" before the crash, but he has since been hospitalized for severe depression. He has also developed aggression issues and has recently faced criminal charges. Warren is currently under house arrest for six months.

By visiting the RADD Web site (http://www.radd.org), you can obtain information on how to order the DVD and an array of downloadable resources. Research shows that videos like *Smashed* can make a powerful impression on young minds. However, longer-lasting effects on teens can be accomplished by coupling the video with an educational session following the viewing of the video. A toolkit available on the RADD Web site offers such resources as a discussion guide, lesson plan, posters, pre- and post-viewing questionnaires, and follow-up activities. It also provides information on how to organize a speakers' panel and how to get local media coverage.

GRIEF AND HEALING

If you have survived a drunk-driving crash, you are probably happy and relieved. But your feelings may be more complicated than that. You may feel guilty if a loved one was hurt and you were not. You may feel anger toward the drunk driver who caused the crash. Maybe you were in the car with the drunk driver, and he or she is your relative or friend. It can be hard to forgive someone when he or she had put your life at risk.

Whether you are a victim or a loved one of a victim, it is important to get help dealing with your feelings. Professionals such as school counselors, social workers, and therapists are trained to help people work through powerful emotions like grief, guilt, and anger. Or, you might feel more comfortable turning to a favorite teacher, coach, or religious leader. Talking about your feelings will be difficult, but it may help. Try not to shut out family and friends. It may seem as if nobody understands what you are going through, but people do want to help.

Drunk driving victims and offenders often go through a long healing and recovery process. It may help to talk with a counselor, attend a support group, or participate in a community event.

If someone you love was killed in a drunk-driving crash, you may experience many painful emotions. You probably feel intense sadness because that person is gone and intense anger toward the drunk driver. If it was your loved one who was driving drunk, you might feel angry with him or her. You might be ashamed that your loved one caused others to be hurt. If you knew that your loved one was too drunk to drive, you probably feel guilty about that, too. You might even feel guilty that you are still alive.

Perhaps your loved one did not die but is permanently disabled after a drunk-driving crash. This is also a very emotionally stressful situation. You are happy the person is alive, but it is difficult to see him or her disabled. You might even feel resentful that you now have to do many things that your loved one cannot do for himself or herself.

Support groups, whether in-person or online, provide a place for you to talk to others who have experienced similar tragedies. There are support groups for people who have lost a loved one. There are also support groups for people who are related to alcoholics or have been affected by alcohol.

TURNING TRAGEDY INTO A TEACHABLE MOMENT

Sometimes, positive things can come out of grief. Mothers Against Drunk Driving (MADD) is one example. Candy Lightner founded MADD in 1980 after her daughter Cari was killed by a drunk driver. She turned her grief into positive steps by pursuing stricter laws and punishments for drunk drivers. Soon after the founding of MADD, friends of Cari organized SADD (Students Against Destructive Decisions; formerly Students Against Driving Drunk). That marked the beginning of teenagers' involvement in the fight against the fatal combination of alcohol and driving.

NOYS is a collaborative network of national organizations, federal agencies, and business and industry members, working together to promote youth safety and health. Both MADD and SADD are members, along with nearly forty other organizations that focus on youth health and safety. YOUTH-Turn, an online tool sponsored by NOYS, is a resource that helps teens and community members turn adversity into educational and constructive opportunities. The goal is to prevent similar tragedies from happening to others. This online tool can be found at http://www.noys.org.

The next chapter is devoted to ideas that teens can implement to help combat the nationwide epidemic of underage drinking and drinking and driving.

CHAPTER 6

Teens who are angered and sickened by the unnecessary and violent deaths of friends and family members continue to organize peer groups to fight back against drunk drivers. Many wonder how they can help curb the underage drinking and impaired driving problem that afflicts today's teens. This chapter offers suggestions about how teens can help.

JOIN A PEER ORGANIZATION

One way to help with the issue of drinking and driving is to join a peer group, such as SADD. Originally, the mission of SADD was to help young people say "No" to drinking and driving. Today, the mission is to provide students with the best prevention tools possible to deal with underage drinking, drug use, impaired driving, and other destructive decisions. SADD students focus on underage drinking, other drug use, risky and impaired driving, teen violence, and teen suicide.

First, check to see if your high school has an active SADD chapter. If not, gather a group of interested and dedicated classmates. Contact the SADD national office by visiting http://www.sadd.org and register your chapter. The Web site

The SADD Web site (http://www.sadd.org) provides information about organizing a chapter, listings of local and national events, newsletters, campaigns, and other resources.

will provide you with information kits, parent contracts, and other products to help you start a chapter in your high school or town. Exploring SADD's Web site is the best way to find information and resources for getting started and to learn how to utilize SADD campaigns and other tools.

MADD is a nationwide movement that has publicized the need for change in our drunk-driving laws. It has succeeded in achieving major legislative changes. MADD'S achievements include:

- Passage of the National Minimum Drinking Age Act
- Stiffer fines and jail sentences for driving while intoxicated
- Lobbying for a national .08 BAC per se law
- Lobbying for a federal zero tolerance law

In 1996, MADD opened up a new division, Youth in Action (YIA). In this division, teams look for community solutions. Examples include cracking down on stores that do not check IDs, asking police officers to do more than simply pour out the beer and send teens home, and stopping adults who buy alcohol for teens. Teams focus on laws and policies that affect people's behavior.

If you are interested in starting a YIA team, visit the Web site at http://www.youthinaction.org. You can check to see if there is already a team in your area. Sometimes, YIA teams coexist with local MADD chapters, so check the MADD Web site as well (http://www. madd.org in the United States and http://www.madd.ca in Canada). To start a YIA team, you need at least one responsible, committed adult and youths in grades nine through twelve.

BE A DESIGNATED DRIVER

If you drink or hang out with people who do, protect yourself by using the designated driver system. The designated driver is someone who volunteers to drive on an occasion when others will be drinking. In Sweden and

England, where this idea started, designated drivers put their car keys in their empty glass so that no one would serve them alcohol.

Having a designated driver ensures that everyone will have a safe ride home. At the next party, someone else from the group takes his or her turn being the designated driver. The driver must be someone you can trust so that when the designated driver says he or she hasn't had anything to drink, you know it is the truth.

People who say, "Well, I haven't had *that* much to drink. I can still drive," are a dangerous choice. The social drinker, as well as the alcoholic, can be a menace on the road. Social drinkers can be impaired because their judgment, reaction time, and coordination are affected. The safest way to drive home from a party is with a completely sober driver.

Sign a Teen/Parent Pact

A pact is an agreement that both teens and parents can live with and will follow through on, if the need arises. The teen and his or her parents sign a formal, written agreement that acknowledges the potential problem in drinking and driving. It also states that you both agree to do something about it. For example, the teen can agree to call a parent to pick him or her up any time the teen faces a risky situation. With a teen/parent pact, teens can face a potentially dangerous situation with confidence, knowing they have parental support in dealing with it. This can alleviate the pressure to get into a car with a drunk driver. The contract must also address situations in which the teen is the one who has had too much to drink and is driving and responsible for others.

The other side of the coin is a clause in the contract in which the parents agree to the same conditions: that the mother or father won't drink and drive or be a passenger in a car with a drunk driver. SADD has created a pact called the "Contract for Life" that a teenager can sign along with his or her parents. The young person's agreement and the parent's agreement look like this:

YOUNG PERSON'S AGREEMENT:

I recognize that there are many potentially destructive decisions I face every day and commit to you that I will do everything in my power to avoid making decisions that will jeopardize my health, my safety and overall well-being, or your trust in me. I understand the dangers associated with the use of alcohol and drugs and the destructive behaviors often associated with impairment.

By signing below, I pledge my best effort to remain free from alcohol and drugs; I agree that I will never drive under the influence; I agree that I will never ride with an impaired driver; and I agree that I will always wear a seat belt.

Finally, I agree to call you if I am ever in a situation that threatens my safety and to communicate with you regularly about issues of importance to both of us.

Parent's (or Caring Adult's) Agreement:

I am committed to you and to your health and safety. By signing below, I pledge to do everything in my power to understand and communicate with you about the many difficult and potentially destructive decisions you face.

Further, I agree to provide for your safe, sober transportation home if you are ever in a situation that threatens your safety and to defer discussions about that situation until a time when we can both have a discussion in a calm and caring manner.

I also pledge to you that I will not drive under the influence of alcohol or drugs, I will always seek safe, sober transportation home, and I will always wear a seat belt.

Working out a contract enables teens and parents to open the door to deeper trust and communication. It also lets teens see that parents can have similar problems. Equal responsibilities, with no double standards, are the goals of a successful teen/parent pact.

Contracts and pacts can allow teens to talk about their fears and what is really going on in their lives. They can also keep a cloak of parental protection around teens at a time when they often resist parental interference. In addition, they give parents a chance to talk about their own concerns and show their love.

ASK DR. JAN, PSYCHOLOGIST

First name: Sara

Question:
I'm a junior, and I think that drinking and driving among teens is a problem at my school. I'd like to get involved in a student group, but I'm not sure what difference I can make when it seems that anyone who's anyone drinks.

Answer:
It is quite common that high school students believe that most of their peers are experimenting with alcohol as well as engaging in other risk behaviors. In fact, it is not true. Every two years, most states conduct an anonymous survey of high school students in order to look at trends for a variety of risk behaviors. In the 2009 Youth Risk Behavior Surveillance Survey, students were asked about alcohol use. For example, when asked about binge drinking (having five or more drinks in a row within a couple of hours), only 24 percent said they had engaged in the behavior during the thirty days before the survey. This means the majority of high school students (76 percent) did not binge drink. While too many high school students (42 percent) indicated that they had at least one drink during the thirty days before the survey, still the majority of students (58 percent) did not drink.

Social norming is an effort to educate people about these kinds of misperceptions because when students mistakenly believe that "everybody does it," it actually increases the chances that they will do it as well. On the flip side, when teens learn the truth—that most other teens practice healthy behaviors—they are likely to drink less. That's why there are social norming campaigns at high schools across the country to educate students about the true facts regarding risk behaviors. Similarly, you and other students in your school can use social norming strategies to help others stay safe.

While you might feel helpless regarding getting involved in your local student group, there is actually a lot that you can do at your school to help fellow students learn the facts about alcohol use in your state. To find out about Youth Risk Behavior Surveillance Survey results in your community, go to http://www.apps.nccd.cdc.gov/youthonline. You can click on your state and get the facts about alcohol use and other risk behaviors.

Ask a Question

Do you have a question that you would like answered? E-mail your question to Dr. Jan at drjan@rosenpub.com. If your question is selected, it will appear on the Teen Health & Wellness Web site in "Dr. Jan's Corner."

If you have an urgent question on a health or wellness issue, we strongly encourage you to call a hotline to speak to a qualified professional or speak to a trusted adult, such as a parent, teacher, or guidance counselor. You can find hotlines listed in the For More Information section of this book, or at www.teenhealthandwellness.com/static/hotlines.

However, there must be a sincere effort on both sides to maintain the agreement. If the contract is regarded as permission to get wasted and then call your parents to bail you out, the agreement is worthless. The contract is your agreement to act responsibly so that your parents can have more trust in you. That is the goal. The more trust you earn, the more freedom you will get. Isn't that worth it?

UTILIZE A SAFE RIDE PROGRAM OR PARENT TAXIS

Safe ride programs offer rides home to teens that don't want to ride with someone who has been drinking. Many local organizations, cities, and college campuses have utilized this kind of program.

There is a lot of preparation for safe rides, and some liability is involved, so you'll need help and supervision to create a program. Enlisting the aid of a local service organization may get you off to a good start.

Holiday weekends, proms, graduations, and parties are important times to offer safe rides. Some communities plan to provide rides on Friday and Saturday nights from 10 PM to 3 AM. Using cell phones and even walkie-talkies, parents and other adults in the community can get involved. It is a good idea for adults to drive in teams of two or three. Drivers should keep records of picked-up

Young people can take action in the community by organizing a safe ride or parent taxi program. Plan for alcohol-free events, especially at high-risk times such as prom and graduation.

teens, times, and addresses. It is important to set up guidelines for confidentiality and to use seat belts and safe cars.

For a more informal plan, several families can set up pacts to provide "parent taxis." Maybe your best friend's father is willing to be on duty this weekend for your friends in case a safe ride is needed after a party or a concert. Next weekend could be your mother's or older brother's turn. Most families are glad to work out this kind of arrangement if you ask and set up some guidelines beforehand.

PLAN FOR A SAFE PROM AND GRADUATION

Organize an alcohol and safety program to keep teens safe during prom and graduation time. Many schools, including Acton-Boxborough Regional High School in Massachusetts and Pecos High School in Maine, offer an all-night, drug- and alcohol-free event on graduation night. Programs like these have received much support and donations from parents, businesses, and communities.

Get your student council or SADD chapter to monitor and promote this worthwhile project. Here are some ideas:

- Give information over the school's public announcement system or Web site.
- Have kids sign pledges not to drink and drive or get into a car with a driver who has been drinking.

- Set up a safe ride system for prom and graduation.
- Organize fun middle-of-the-night activities at a local school, community center, pool, or athletic facility, with adult supervision.
- Promote seat belt use and publicize the dangers of distracted driving.
- Make posters of slogans repeating the message, "Stay alive, don't drink and drive."
- Print up a list of local limousine companies with their costs.

Remember that many national nonprofit organizations offer online toolkits to aid you with planning for your safe prom and graduation.

Start a Media or Internet Campaign

Public service information is in demand. Create radio and local cable TV announcements about staying straight, staying alive, and buckling up. When teens pose a responsible pitch to the local media, they can usually get on the radio or television. Teens helping teens makes news.

Work to get the names of drunk drivers published in the newspaper. This has been successful in some towns because teens and adults become a little more cautious if their "secret" of a drunk-driving arrest and license revocation may get out.

Utilize technology. Get a viral campaign going in your school. Have parents, teachers, administrators, and teens

A graduate of a Florida high school, who lost his left leg after being hit by a drunk driver in 2009, returns to speak at a prom safety program for younger students.

write e-mails and send petitions to the elected officials and judges in your community. Express your concerns about drinking and driving and ask for public officials' help in battling the problem. Depending on the issue, many organizations will have sample e-mails available as models.

Promote a campaign through the many technology outlets that exist. If you cannot think of a campaign, use existing campaigns from SADD ("21 or Bust" or "Think About It . . . Is It Worth The Risk?") and NHTSA ("You Drink, You Drive, You Lose" or "Over the Limit, Under Arrest"). Using national campaigns usually allows you to access online resources. Some ideas for promoting your campaign include:

- E-mails
- Text messages
- Social networking sites where you can start a new group and create events
- Video clips
- Flash games and other apps for download

Some possible events to organize, which might attract media coverage, are a large rally or an assembly with a panel of speakers. Panelists to consider include drunk-driving victims, teens, emergency room nurses or physicians, other health professionals or experts, law enforcement officials, and parents. Plan for a car crash demonstration. Host a screening of *Smashed*. Be sure that adults are involved, but make it a teen-led initiative.

TARGET YOUNGER STUDENTS

Run poster and slogan contests in the elementary and junior high schools in your town. Interact with younger students and teach them what you know about drugs and alcohol. Solicit local businesses and law enforcement agencies to donate prizes (such as free pizza or movie tickets) to entice the younger kids to make a commitment to stay away from alcohol.

Make sure to get organized before you pitch your ideas to your school superintendent and principal. Presenting a responsible, organized plan will earn you respect and the green light to go ahead with your project.

PROTECT YOURSELF AND OTHERS

There are ways that you can spot an impaired or drunk driver. Knowing how to recognize the signals and react to them may help protect you from being involved in an alcohol-related crash.

A person swerving or not driving in a straight path on the correct side of the road is someone to avoid. He or she may be driving on the shoulder or may cross into the opposite lane before pulling back to the correct side. Misjudging turns, either by unusually wide turns or abrupt or illegal turns, is another sign. An impaired driver may also respond slowly to traffic signals, straddle or drive on the centerline, or speed up or slow down for no reason. Forgetting to put on headlights and tailgating are other warning signs. Impaired drivers often forget to use their turn signals or are not able to judge stopping distances accurately. Don't always trust other drivers on the road, especially late at night or on weekends. Be safe, not sorry.

Let's say you are driving with your learner's permit, and your friend, who is a licensed driver, is in the passenger seat. Ahead is a flashy new Corvette, but it seems to be having trouble staying on the right side of the road. Every once in a while, it goes onto the shoulder and then pulls back toward the centerline.

What do you do?

Instead of driving up to investigate what may be happening, hang back and maintain a safe following distance

Young people have the power to make a difference. Be a role model to fellow peers; practice being a safe and smart driver.

(one car length for each 10 miles [16 km] per hour you are driving). Stay away from that car and its driver.

Be careful at those blinking-light intersections that are so easy to cruise through. Even if you have the yellow blinking light as opposed to the red blinking light, you can slow down almost to a stop and check out the crossroad.

If you see someone coming at you over the center-line, the best thing to do is sound your horn, flash your lights, and pull over to the right. Always make sure you use a seat belt, and lock the doors for safety. Next, you should pull over and call the police to report the driver. As accurately as you can, give a description of the car, its license plate number, and the direction in which it's headed. Even though you may be shaken, do the best you can. The police can follow up on your information. You may save someone's life.

Some teens feel that they have no power, and that they could never change the world. But the truth is, you can. Volunteering in a peer-led organization, helping teens get safe rides, maintaining your own values, and promoting healthy habits to younger kids can make a difference. It can save lives, including your own.

ABOUT DR. JAN

Dr. Jan Hittelman is a licensed psychologist with over twenty years of experience working with teens, children, adults, and families in a variety of settings.

In addition to clinical practices in California, Colorado, and New York, he has specialized in program development in partnership with school systems, psychiatric hospitals, correctional facilities and the courts, outpatient settings, residential treatment facilities, and private nonprofit organizations.

He founded Compass House, a nonprofit counseling collaborative for teens and their families. He launched Boulder Psychological Services in 2007.

Dr. Hittelman also authors a monthly newspaper column entitled "Surviving the Teenage Years" in the *Boulder Daily Camera*, writes monthly columns for the Boulder Valley School District under the sponsorship of the Parent Engagement Network, and publishes an online question-and-answer column for teens in the Rosen Publishing Group's online resource Teen Health & Wellness.

Teen Health & Wellness: Real Life, Real Answers (*http://www.teenhealthandwellness.com*) is a database designed for teens on issues relating to health, fitness, alcohol, drugs, mental health, family life, and much more. Check your school or local library for access.

GLOSSARY

alcohol abuse A pattern of alcohol use in which the person continues to drink despite social and interpersonal consequences and alcohol-related legal problems.

alcohol dependence A pattern of alcohol use in which the person shows tolerance, withdrawal symptoms, lack of control when drinking, preoccupation with alcohol, and use of alcohol despite physical and psychological consequences.

alcohol poisoning An overdose of alcohol in which the blood alcohol level rises to a danger point and the body's involuntary functions are interrupted or stopped. The person can die from choking on vomit, loss of breath or heartbeat, seizures, or cardiac arrest. A quick method to identify poisoning is the "ten rule": fewer than ten breaths taken in one minute and more than ten seconds elapsing between inhalation and exhalation.

alcopop A flavored alcoholic beverage.

blood alcohol content (BAC) The concentration of alcohol in the blood, used as a measure of the degree of intoxication in an individual.

central nervous system The part of the vertebrate nervous system consisting of the brain and spinal cord; it controls and coordinates the activities of the body.

cognizance Awareness.

coma A state of deep, prolonged unconsciousness that results from injury, disease, or poison. The person cannot be roused and does not respond to external stimuli.

denial Refusal to recognize or acknowledge painful truths (e.g., the relationship between one's drinking and severe life problems).

depressant An agent, especially a drug, which decreases the rate of vital activities in the body.

fatality A death resulting from an accident or disaster.

impaired Functioning poorly or inadequately; intoxicated by alcohol or drugs.

intervention The act of interfering with a process, especially to prevent harm or improve functioning.

intoxicated Affected by alcohol or drugs to the point where physical and mental control is markedly diminished; drunk.

motor vehicle crash A collision between an automobile, truck, bus, motorcycle, or motorized bike and another vehicle, pedestrian, animal, road debris, or other obstacle.

negligence Failure to exercise the degree of care that the law requires for the protection of other people.

passenger Any occupant of a motor vehicle who is not the driver.

peer pressure Social pressure by members of one's peer group, encouraging a person to change his or her attitudes, values, or behaviors in order to conform to group norms.

revocation The act of withdrawing or canceling.

sober Not intoxicated or drunk; not under the influence of alcohol or drugs.

sobriety checkpoint A roadblock where law enforcement officials stop vehicles according to a predetermined pattern and investigate the possibility of impaired driving.

tolerance A condition in which higher doses of a drug are required to produce the same effect as experienced initially.

treatment Activities designed to change a pattern of unhealthy behavior, such as that which occurs with alcohol dependence or addiction. Activities can include detoxification, counseling, and education.

zero tolerance The policy of applying penalties to even minor infringements of a law in order to reinforce its importance.

FOR MORE INFORMATION

ASPIRA National Office
1444 I Street NW, Suite 800
Washington, DC 20005
(202) 835-3600
Web site: http://www.aspira.org

This nonprofit organization is dedicated to developing the educational and leadership capacity of Hispanic youth. Programming efforts include traffic safety issues, such as seat belt use and alcohol awareness.

The BACCHUS Network
P.O. Box 100430
Denver, CO 80250-0430
(303) 871-0901
Web site: http://www.bacchusnetwork.org

This nonprofit university and community-based network focuses on comprehensive health and safety initiatives. Using a peer educator approach, BACCHUS provides the college campus and community with programming on topics such as alcohol awareness and impaired driving prevention.

Mothers Against Drunk Driving (MADD)
511 East John Carpenter Freeway, Suite 700
Irving, TX 75062
(800) GET-MADD [438-6233]
Web site: http://www.madd.org

For more than thirty years, MADD has been fighting to stop drunk driving, support the victims of this violent crime, and prevent underage drinking. It has been effective in raising public awareness of the issue and in changing legislation.

National Council on Alcoholism and Drug Dependence (NCADD)

244 East 58th Street, 4th Floor
New York, NY 10022
(212) 269-7797
Web site: http://www.ncadd.org

NCADD's mission is to fight the stigma and the disease of alcoholism and other drug addictions. The organization's Web site contains information about programs, services, and advocacy opportunities, as well as treatment centers and recovery resources.

National Highway Traffic Safety Administration (NHTSA)

1200 New Jersey Avenue SE
West Building
Washington, DC 20590
(888) 327-4236
Web site: http://www.nhtsa.gov

This federal agency, part of the Department of Transportation, was established to carry out safety and consumer programs. The Web site offers extensive information, toolkits, and national data on topics such as teen driving, impaired driving, distracted driving, and vehicle safety.

National Organizations for Youth Safety (NOYS)

7371 Atlas Walk Way, #109
Gainesville, VA 20155
(828) FOR-NOYS [367-6697]

Web site: http://www.noys.org

NOYS is a network of national organizations, federal agencies, and business and industry members that serve youth. It provides the public with useful resources on underage drinking and driving, substance abuse, and many other issues related to youth safety and health.

National Road Safety Foundation (NRSF)

18 East 50th Street
New York, NY 10022
(866) SAFE-PATH [723-3728]
Web site: http://www.nrsf.org

NRSF produces documentaries, educational programs, and public service campaigns for broadcast and use in safety, education, and enforcement programs. It offers its productions free of charge.

SADD Alberta

P.O. Box 7220
Calgary, AB T2P 3M1
Canada
(403) 313-SADD
Web site: http://www.saddalberta.com

SADD works to unite Canadian youth in the stand against impaired driving. Its Web site offers chapter information, conferences, promotional material, and links to SADD groups in other provinces.

Transport Canada

330 Sparks Street
Ottawa, ON K1A 0N5
Canada

(613) 990-2309
Web site: http://www.tc.gc.ca

Transport Canada, a division of the government of Canada, promotes efficient, safe, and secure transportation systems and environmental responsibility. Its Web site offers information and resources on all modes of transportation.

WEB SITES

Due to the changing nature of Internet links, Rosen Publishing has developed an online list of Web sites related to the subject of this book. This site is updated regularly. Please use this link to access the list:

http://www.rosenlinks.com/411/dri

FOR FURTHER READING

Aksomitis, Linda. *Teen Driving* (Issues That Concern You). Farmington Hills, MI: Greenhaven Press, 2009.

Aretha, David. *On the Rocks: Teens and Alcohol*. New York, NY: Franklin Watts, 2007.

Aronson, Sarah. *Head Case*. New York, NY: Roaring Brook Press, 2007.

Cefrey, Holly. *Frequently Asked Questions About Drinking and Driving* (FAQ: Teen Life). New York, NY: Rosen Publishing Group, 2009.

Friedman, Lauri S. *Alcohol* (Introducing Issues with Opposing Viewpoints). Farmington Hills, MI: Greenhaven Press, 2010.

Greenfield, Beth. *Ten Minutes from Home: A Memoir*. New York, NY: Harmony Books, 2010.

Kuhn, Cynthia, Scott Swartzwelder, Wilkie Wilson, Leigh Heather Wilson, and Jeremy Foster. *Buzzed: The Straight Facts About the Most Used and Abused Drugs from Alcohol to Ecstasy*. 3rd ed. New York, NY: W. W. Norton, 2008.

Parks, Peggy J. *Drunk Driving* (Compact Research Series). San Diego, CA: ReferencePoint Press, 2010.

Radev, Anna, and KidsPeace. *I've Got This Friend Who: Advice for Teens and Their Friends on Alcohol, Drugs, Eating Disorders, Risky Behaviors, and More*. Center City, MN: Hazelden, 2007.

Roza, Greg. *Frequently Asked Questions About Driving and the Law* (FAQ: Teen Life). New York, NY: Rosen Publishing Group, 2010.

Stewart, Gail B. *Drowning in a Bottle: Teens and Alcohol Abuse* (What's the Issue?). Mankato, MN: Compass Point Books, 2009.

Strasser, Todd. *The Accident*. New York, NY: Delacorte Press, 1988.

Van Tuyl, Christine. *Drunk Driving* (Issues That Concern You). Farmington Hills, MI: Greenhaven Press, 2006.

Volkmann, Chris, and Toren Volkmann. *From Binge to Blackout: A Mother and Son Struggle with Teen Drinking*. New York, NY: New American Library, 2006.

Wilson, Mike. *Drunk Driving* (Introducing Issues with Opposing Viewpoints). Farmington Hills, MI: Greenhaven Press, 2007.

Zailckas, Koren. *Smashed: Story of a Drunken Girlhood*. New York, NY: Viking, 2005.

INDEX

ABOUT THE AUTHORS

Valerie Mendralla, RN, MPH, CHES, CADC, has worked on youth health and safety issues for over ten years. She has held leadership positions with The BACCHUS Network and National Organizations for Youth Safety. Ms. Mendralla received her master of public health degree from the University of Minnesota and her bachelor of science degree from the University of Wisconsin-Parkside.

Janet Grosshandler served as a high school guidance counselor in Jackson, New Jersey, for twenty-eight years. She is the author of ten guidance books for teenagers.

PHOTO CREDITS

Cover, pp. 1, 4, 7, 24, 27, 104 Shutterstock; pp. 9, 51 National Highway Traffic Safety Administration; pp. 12, 66, 94, 106 Courtesy of Jan S. Hittelman, Ph.D.; p. 14 SW Productions/Photodisc/Getty Images; p. 20 National Institute on Alcohol Abuse and Alcoholism; pp. 22 Campus Alcohol Abuse Prevention Center, Virginia Tech; p. 29 Fstop/Photodisc/Getty Images; p. 33 Robyn Beck/AFP/ Getty Images; p. 35 Michael Krasowitz/Getty Images; p. 37 National Institute on Drug Abuse/NIH; p. 47 Thinkstock/Comstock/ Getty Images; p. 53 Design Pics/ Colleen Cahill/Getty Images; p. 57 Toshifumi Kitamura/ AFP/Getty Images; pp. 60–61 Joe Raedle/Getty Image News/ Getty Images; pp. 70–71, 84-85, 97 © AP Images; p. 89 SADD, Inc.; pp. 100–101 © St. Petersburg Times/Brendan Fitterer/The Image Works.

Editor: Andrea Sclarow; Photo Researcher: Marty Levick